HUMANISM AS THE NEXT STEP

LLOYD L. MORAIN, president of the American Humanist Association, studied under Alfred Korzybski, Bertrand Russell, and Hans Reichenbach. A former personnel consultant, he is now a personal business advisor in San Francisco, and a director of twelve industrial, public utility, and financial corporations.

His wife, MARY MORAIN, is a director of the International Humanist and Ethical Union. Holder of a master's degree in political science from the University of Chicago, she has been both a social worker and a college teacher, and has served as a vice-president of the League of Women Voters of Boston and of the Planned Parenthood League of Massachusetts.

HUMANISM
AS THE NEXT STEP

An Introduction
for Liberal Protestants, Catholics, and Jews

By LLOYD *and* MARY MORAIN

THE BEACON PRESS · BOSTON

Library of Congress Catalog Card Number: 54–6161
Printed in U.S.A.

Contents

HUMANISM AS THE NEXT STEP

CHAPTER ONE

The Fourth Faith

A Growing Movement

Every year more men and women of all races are calling themselves humanists. For them the old orthodoxies have lost significance. They are finding satisfaction in the positive, constructive point of view of humanism. In Europe and the Americas it is coming to be known as the fourth faith. It shares much with the philosophies and religions of the East as well as of the West.

Throughout the ages religions of many kinds have contained a common spirit. We can see this in their scriptures.

In Brahmanism we find: " This is the sum of duty: Do naught unto others which would cause you pain if done to you " (*Mahabharata,* 5, 1517).

In Buddhism: " Hurt not others in ways that you yourself would find hurtful " (*Udana-Varga* 5, 18).

In Christianity: " All things whatsoever ye would that man should do to you, do ye even so to them: for this is the Law and the Prophets " (*Matthew* 7, 12).

In Confucianism: " Is there one maxim which ought to be acted upon throughout one's whole life? Surely it is the maxim of loving-kindness: Do not unto others what you would not have them do unto you " (*Analects* 15, 23).

In Islam: "No one of you is a believer until he desires for his brother that which he desires for himself" (*Sunnah*).

In Judaism: "What is hateful to you, do not to your fellowman. That is the entire Law; all the rest is commentary" (*Talmud, Shabbat* 31d).

In Taoism: "Regard your neighbor's gain as your own gain, and your neighbor's loss as your own loss" (*T'ai Shang Kan Ying P'ien*).

Upon this common ethical basis have been built varying religious practices and diverse theological beliefs.

Down through the ages men have been seeking a universal religion or way of life. They are still seeking. Throughout the world there are wide cultural variations. Ways of worship, rituals, symbols, and sacraments are different. Humanism, built squarely on the universal idea of brotherhood, upon the golden rule, shows promise of becoming a great world faith.

Humanists are content with fixing their attention on this life and on this earth. Theirs is a religion without a God, divine revelation, or sacred scriptures. Yet theirs is a faith rich in feeling and understanding. They see sorrows and joys, tragedies and triumphs, touching every fiber of human life. They experience wholesome humility as they venture forward with their fellow men into the as-yet-unknown.

We may now note several facts about this rapidly growing philosophy and religion.

(1) It has developed in response to the spiritual needs and aspirations of people in different parts of the world.

(2) It contains an ethical core similar to that of many religions and philosophies.

(3) It is free from divisive doctrines about the unknown, deity, revelation, sacred scriptures, rituals, sacraments, formal theology, and such befuddling ideas as the radical separation of either the world or the individual into matter and spirit.

(4) It is a philosophy of men's relations to one another and to nature, rather than of men's relations to deity.

Built on this fresh, vital basis it is little wonder that humanism has called forth accelerated world-wide interest. In 1952, for the first time, representatives from humanist groups in many countries met in Holland and formed the International Humanist and Ethical Union. Julian Huxley, a biologist and the first Director-General of Unesco, served as president. He is among those who believe that humanism will be the world's next great faith.

Here in the United States the number of humanist groups has doubled in each of the past several years. Some of these groups, for example, many of the Unitarian Fellowships, are functioning under the auspices of a liberal religious denomination. Each year more and more Protestants, Catholics, and Jews, as well as many without any previous religious affiliation, are coming to follow as their own this way of life.

This faith is held by a large number of individuals who have made or are making solid contributions to human welfare and understanding. Among distinguished humanists of the recent past are Edwin G. Conklin, John Dewey, Horace Fries, John Galsworthy, Frederick J. Gould, Sir Richard Gregory, John A. Hobson, James H. Leuba, Sinclair Lewis, Eduard C. Lindeman, F. S. Marvin, Arthur B. Moehlman, Hans Reichenbach, Porter Sargent, and George Santayana. Their influence has spread in countless ways and has given humanism a powerful momentum. In many respects humanism's strength is found, as any list will show, in the high proportion of eminent leaders and thinkers who today hold this faith. Yet to an increasing degree those following this way of life represent a cross section of the American population.

We believe that it will help the reader to understand the movement if we list some of the people who have expressed ideas consistent with the rich and varied humanist view.

Those who have contributed to the advancement of human welfare and understanding on the international scene include Brock Chisholm, Julian Huxley, Sir Arthur Keith, Lord Boyd Orr, and Gerald Wendt.

Some of those contributing to arts and letters are Conrad Aiken, A. J. Ayer, Eleanor D. Berman, Van Wyck Brooks, M. L. Burnet, Witter Bynner, Blodwen Davies, LeGarde S. Doughty, Dorothy Canfield Fisher, James T. Farrell, Charles I. Glicksberg, Henry Hazlitt, Llewellyn Jones, Joseph Wood Krutch, Thomas Mann, Herbert J. Muller, Gilbert Murray, Priscilla Robertson, Jules Romains, Allen Walker Read, and Miriam de Ford Shipley.

The list of philosophers could become very long because various philosophic positions emerge into humanism. The point of view known as " scientific humanism " has been developed very largely among this group. Such philosophers include Van Meter Ames, C. E. Ayres, Arthur Bentley, Brand Blanshard, Boyd H. Bode, Fortunato Brancatisano, Rudolf Carnap, Irwin Edman, Herbert Feigl, Philipp Frank, George R. Geiger, Sidney Hook, Horace M. Kallen, Corliss Lamont, Harold A. Larrabee, J. A. Leighton, Charles Mayer, D. Michael Morandini, Max Otto, John Herman Randall, Jr., Joseph Ratner,

Oliver L. Reiser, M. N. Roy, Roy Wood Sellars, Surindar S. Suri, Charles Morris, and Gardner Williams. Other philosophers, including A. J. Bahm, Rubin Gotesky, James L. Jarrett, Jr., Keith McGary, Francis Myers, Donald A. Piatt, Sidney Ratner, and Philip Phenix, have helped with the editing of *The Humanist*.

Many teachers of religion, liberal ministers, and ethical leaders are identified with the fourth faith. Educators in this field include J. A. C. F. Auer, Alfred S. Cole, A. Eustace Haydon, Charles H. Lyttle, and Conrad Moehlman. Unitarian, Universalist, and Humanist Society ministers among many others include T. C. Abell, E. Burdette Backus, L. M. Birkhead, Raymond B. Bragg, John Brogden, Edwin T. Buehrer, Fred I Cairns, Ernest Caldecott, David Cole, Dale DeWitt, Albert C. Dieffenbach, John Gardner Greene, William D. Hammond, Albert Harkins, John H. Hershey, Randall Hilton, E. S. Hodgin, William P. Jenkins, John MacKinnon, James W. MacKnight, Philip Mayer, Kenneth L. Patton, Charles Francis Potter, Tracy M. Pullman, Curtis W. Reese, Peter Sansom, Philip Schug, Clinton Lee Scott, Harold Scott, Fred Shorter, Carl A. Storm, Kenneth C. Walker, David Rhys Williams, and Edwin H. Wilson. Ethical leaders identified with the position include Harold Blackham, Arthur E. Briggs, Percival Chubb, James F. Hornbach, J. Hutton Hynd, R. Lester Mondale, and George O'Dell. Although they tend to express themselves within the traditional symbols, numerous rabbis in the non-orthodox Jewish groups — the Reformed, the Reconstructionist, and the Conservative, express interest in the movement. Of these Mordecai Kaplan, Bertram Korn, and the late Solomon Goldman are among the most distinguished.

Rudolf Dreikurs, Erich Fromm, and Karl A. Menninger, are among the psychiatrists. Educators and social scientists make up the largest group. Here we might mention George E. Axtelle, Read Bain, Harry Elmer Barnes, Frederick H. Burkhardt, Nathaniel Cantor, Wallace O. Fenn, Virginia Flemming, Frank H. Hankins, S. I. Hayakawa, John C. Kidneigh, William Heard Kilpatrick, Alfred McClung Lee, William G. Rice, Jacob Saposnekow, John R. Seeley, Clarence Senior, George Simpson, Mark Starr, George D. Stoddard, E. L. Talbert, Harold Taylor, V. T. Thayer, Claude W. Thompson, Norman Torrey, and E. C. Vanderlaan.

Scientists, engineers, and architects who are known as humanists include Malcolm H. Bissell, Anton J. Carlson, Saul Dushman, Ralph W. Girard, C. Judson Herrick, Clyde Kluckhohn, Arthur E. Morgan, Rexford Newcomb, Harold R. and Helen Rafton, Karl Sax, Paul Schweikher, Maurice B. Visscher, and Willis R. Whitney.

Among those working largely within free thought groups to bring about a more humanist emphasis are C. Bradlaugh Bonner, Ira D. Cardiff, George A. Fink, Paul Kinney, Hugh Robert Orr, Mr. and Mrs. Eldon Scholl, and E. L. Dwight Turner.

There are numerous other eminent citizens not easily classified in one or another of the groups we have mentioned. Of these we might list Jessie L. Armstrong, Raymond C. Baumgardner, Warner Clark, Arthur C. Comey, Philip R. Faymonville, Ruby D. Garrett, Edouard Herriot, Harrison Hires, William H. Holly, Roy John, Gordon Kent, Julius Kespohl, J. Jack Lang, Leo Lerner, Clarence H. Low, Vashti McCollum, Robert G. Risk, Jud R. Scholtz, J. Ray Shute, Sherman and Eva Wakefield,

James Peter Warbasse, James H. White, Herbert A. Wise, and Mary Winsor.

That these hundred and eighty leaders of independent mind and spirit should share this common faith attests to its vitality. There are of course varied emphases in humanism and the particular quality of an individual's views will be conditioned, within the very wide limits of this philosophy, by his background, whatever it may be — science, philosophy, business, social work, literature and the arts, liberal religion, free thought, or other area of activity. A few of those individuals mentioned may not apply the humanist label to themselves. In some cases they may point to a particular humanist and say, "I am not that kind of humanist." But would not that also be true of other faiths and philosophies? A few people have labelphobia. Our list is, however, a reasonable cross-section, and most of those mentioned are members of the American Humanist Association. The few who are not, can, by their own writing and declarations, be identified as pursuing this way of life, or as expressing in their published views many humanist principles.

This faith is beginning to make an impact on human affairs. It is a faith appropriate to an age in which men are coming to realize their own strength and worth.

We are living in a time of vigorous protest. We see in many parts of the world agonized efforts on the part of peoples to rule themselves, to democratize their governments. Just as political concepts of divine right and control have been overthrown, so many of the traditional religious and philosophical ideas are being challenged. In many instances people have simply turned away from religious activity. They are doing this even in those countries where to do so brings social disapproval, even ostra-cism. For them no institution or group of people has a corner on wisdom or on high ethical principles. They recognize the whole human family as a great interdepend-ent brotherhood.

People everywhere are coming to realize that science is universal and not localized knowledge or belief. They know that biologists, whether in Bolivia, in Japan, or in Sweden, have a basis of common principles and share the fruits of their knowledge. There is no special kind of Bolivian or Japanese biology which is radically different from Swedish biology. Political leaders in a few nations have tried to shape scientific studies to nationalistic ends but they sooner or later fail in this. People are also com-ing to understand that ethical principles and basic stand-ards of moral conduct have common roots and universal application. It is only natural that those groups who tie these standards into special rituals, religious observances, and theologies are fighting a defensive, losing battle. The human spirit is too vigorous to be kept forever in shackles.

The past few years have seen the formation of humanist groups in nations as different as India and Holland. Or-ganizations in several countries have been started by in-dividuals who had no inkling of the fact that at the same time people in other countries were also starting groups. Men and women of different nations arrived at the same conclusions and proceeded in the same way to give them form.

One difference between the humanist movement in America and in other parts of the world is that in some countries humanism is thought of as a Third Way or third force. That is, it is considered an alternative of belief and

action to the authoritarian political systems on the one
hand and to the traditional religions on the other. Here
in America where we enjoy democratic political freedom
we do not have to seek such an alternative, and so far as
we know this faith is rarely spoken of over here as a Third
Way.

Whether or not there will be humanist halls in every
city of our land and tens of millions of members remains
to be seen. In its present stage of growth the fourth faith
is having a liberalizing influence on many of the traditional religions and philosophies. Within the Unitarian,
Universalist, and Ethical Culture organizations whole congregations are becoming openly humanist. The mounting concern of the Protestant, Catholic, and Jewish cler-
gies over the effect of humanism on some members of
their churches testifies to the appeal and strength of the
fourth faith.

The American Humanist Association helps to bring together humanists wherever they are found. A number
are in liberal churches and enjoy membership in both
their church and the A. H. A. Such humanists take part
in the educational program of the Association which is a
cooperating rather than a competing organization. Human fulfilment is the goal; institutions are instruments of
fulfilment.

Religion and the Religious Attitude

Attempts to ridicule religion or to dismiss it as unimportant rarely meet with any lasting success. For religion
is a vital part of the lives of many of us. It gives every in-
dication of continuing to be so.

Religion has been defined in nearly as many ways as there

have been definers. It is often spoken of as "a system of faith or worship," or as "an awareness or conviction of the existence of a supreme being arousing reverence, love, gratitude, and the will to obey."

Other thoughtful men have given very different definitions. Thomas Paine merely said: "The world is my country, to do good my religion."

A. Eustace Haydon, professor emeritus of comparative religion at the University of Chicago, offers as his definition: "The shared quest of the good life."

Alfred North Whitehead has described it simply as "what the individual does with his solitariness."

To us religion is the creation and pursuit of ideals and the relationship men feel with one another and with the universe. For us religion and theology are not necessarily the same.

Most humanists believe that the ordinary individual can have a religious experience which does not include any supernatural element. Humanists suggest that religious feeling and attitudes have been mistakenly limited. They have been limited to that which is becoming less and less real and meaningful to us — the old theologies and rituals.

John Dewey describes religious attitudes as basically a thoroughgoing and deep-seated harmonizing of the self with the universe. And he further defines religious experience as that which has the power to bring about a deeper and more enduring adjustment to life. Can we not agree with Dewey that everyday life will have more meaning once we realize that religious experiences are a part of its fabric?

Julian Huxley regards the basis of religion as "the consciousness of sanctity in existence, in common things, in events of human life."

Horace M. Kallen, in an address for the " Faith in Action " series of the National Broadcasting Company net-
work, said:

What makes a religious man is not what he believes, but
how he believes in it. A belief becomes religious when a man
makes his total commitment, risks his life, on what he believes.
Now, you might say that the American way is the most com-
prehensive religious way because it insures that freedom of
commitment for all sorts of different beliefs. And that's why
the American way and the Humanist way coincide.

From time immemorial men have related their lives
with the larger life of nature. They wished to feel that
their code of social behavior had something of the sacred
in it. These attitudes have been organized together in
the idea of " God." Yet men can receive these same satisfactions from a philosophy which is not built on the idea
of deity. Men can learn that ideals are in reality useful
goals growing out of human experience and not set apart
from creative life. Men can learn that their lives are
more closely woven into the whole universe than they had
even suspected in the old days. Religion without a supernatural element becomes meaningful and personal.

The endless struggle between science and religion dies
down. The spiritual aspects of life are no longer incon-
sistent and at odds with those things that we can experience
and test. No longer need there be that type of spiritual
realm that does violence to our intelligence and to our
knowledge of the processes of the world.

Humanism as a Philosophy and Religion

Humanism as well as religion has been defined in in-
numerable ways. Many a humanist has made his own
definition. This is a healthful condition. For truths are

not contained within the words of definitions. The value of definitions is in calling attention to relationships or in making appropriate descriptions. The broad general humanist viewpoint, enriched as it is by the insights of people of varying temperaments, cannot even be sketched within a few sentences or paragraphs. As it is a general point of view it is only natural that different people should find different aspects of it particularly significant to them.

Those individuals of more philosophical bent will look to it as a living philosophy. If they are technically trained they may study humanist theories of knowledge and of value. Some whose primary interest is found in current world problems, in building a better, happier human community, naturally think of humanism as a point of view that could bring all the people of the world together. For them it is a challenging call to make full use of all that is in us to build cooperatively a richer human life. The interest of yet another group is in the role of humanism as a champion of the scientific approach as over against the traditional theological one, of democracy over authoritarianism, of common sense over superstition. A fourth group hails it as a means for achieving personal integration, maturity, and freedom. Once these personal values are won, concern in, and action for, the larger social good follows naturally.

Whether or not one looks to humanism as a religion or as a philosophy to live by or as a way of life is, we believe, largely a matter of personal temperament and preference. Those caught up by its religious aspects know that it provides a vibrant, satisfying faith. Those who think of it as a philosophy find it both reasonable and adequate.

One of the great religious humanist pioneers, John H. Dietrich, pointed out:

For centuries the idea of God has been the very heart of religion; it has been said "no God, no religion." But humanism thinks of religion as something very different and far deeper than any belief in God. To it, religion is not the attempt to establish right relations with a supernatural being, but rather the upreaching and aspiring impulse in a human life. It is life striving for its completest fulfillment, and anything which contributes to this fulfillment is religious, whether it be associated with the idea of God or not.

Another humanist pioneer, Charles Francis Potter, defines humanism as, " Faith in the supreme self-perfectibility of the human personality."

Humanism gives to many people the satisfactions which have come to them in the past either from other religions or from other philosophies. In doing this it serves some as a religion, others as a philosophy. Inasmuch as it is both a philosophy and a religion there is no need to deny that it has both functions.

It developed as the scientific viewpoint was grafted upon a philosophy of good will and of confidence in men and nature. It is neither vague nor colorless but positive and dynamic, whether thought of as a religion, a philosophy, or a way of life.

CHAPTER TWO

Forerunners of Humanism

Seven Contributing Ideas

The ideas which make up humanism have developed slowly throughout history and will not fade into oblivion just because people may some day cease to use the term " humanist." Although there were individual humanists in each of the past twenty-five or more centuries, it has been only in the present one that organized groups have developed and that these ideas have been recognized as forming a point of view, an approach to life.

Nothing human is alien to this faith. The entire past of man can be claimed as its tradition. It has been called the oldest and most complete of faiths.

There are, however, certain specific ideas which have gone into the making of modern humanism. Seven of these, although at some points shading into one another, seem to us to stand out.

As a starting point let us take the idea that this life should be experienced deeply, lived fully, with sensitive awareness and appreciation of that which is around us. Artists and explorers, in particular, have had this keen awareness. This idea has long been important in the humanist tradition.

Another idea is that nature is thoroughly worthy of attention, of study. Early philosopher-scientists, among them Aristotle, shaped this notion.

Still another idea is that of confidence in men. For expression of this we are indebted in large measure to the eighteenth-century democrats who had faith that men can control their own destinies.

A fourth idea is that of the equality of rights among men. This is part of the democratic ideal and for it we are again particularly under obligation to the eighteenth-century democrats.

Brotherhood and mutual aid are chosen as a fifth central idea. This important theme lies deep in most religions. Early humanists were exhilarated to see it given a new justification through the work of sociologists and biologists.

A further idea is that of evolution as worked out by nineteenth-century scientists. Early humanists were quick to realize the implications of development through gradual change.

For the seventh and last idea we have chosen the basic rule of science, the need of proving theory by experience. On this principle has been built the whole modern scientific method of verification by experiment. No other idea has been of more practical importance to the humanist movement than this one.

Enthusiasm for Life

Back through the centuries whenever men have enjoyed keenly the sights and sounds and other sensations of the world about them, and enjoyed these for what they were — not because they stood for something else — they were experiencing life humanistically. Whenever they felt keen interest in the drama of human life about them and ardently desired to take part in it they felt as humanists.

The Greek and Roman philosophers Epicurus and Lucretius urged their followers to find happiness in the present world, in nature, and in the affection of friends. During the Renaissance there was a general rebirth of interest in the present, of zest for living.

In each age the work of some artists has revealed the beauty of the world as it is, beauty that might otherwise go unnoticed. Such work has given new insights into the grandeur and meaning of human life as men experience it. Beethoven's fifth and ninth symphonies, Rembrandt's portraits, Shakespeare's plays do this for us.

Men have shown a humanist spirit when they were eager to make their life yet richer and more satisfying, easier, more comfortable, and more stimulating.

Nature Matters

Throughout history a scattering of men have relied on their intelligence and energies to force nature to give up her secrets. They have done this in order to make life more livable, or because of an inspired, disciplined curiosity.

In the humanist tradition are Copernicus, Galileo, and other investigators who, in the face of indifference or hostility, courageously observed, experimented, recorded, and formulated. They took the whole universe as their domain daring to explore the heavens, the earth, and man.

Protagoras, speaking in Greece, 500 B.C., encouraged men to turn their minds to the investigation of what lay about them. " As to the gods," he said, " I have no means of knowing either that they exist or do not exist. For many are the obstacles that impede knowledge, both the obscurity of the questions and the shortness of human life." He it was who gave us that famous dictum: " Man is the measure of all things."

Many centuries later Francis Bacon, leading the revolt against medieval scholasticism, urged men to pursue science.

In philosophy, the materialist and naturalist tradition had sturdy roots in ancient times. Early philosophers basing their systems entirely on the natural world founded these schools of thought. The naturalists emphasized the sufficiency of nature as a framework for thinking. The materialists developed theories of matter little different from those held in this atomic age. Today these have been developed and blended together. However, they had barely survived the rise of the Church and the advent of the Dark Ages. The modern tradition can be traced through Bacon, Spinoza, and Peirce to George H. Mead, John Dewey, Hans Reichenbach, and Arthur Bentley. Modern refinements have been important, but for this school of thought nature as the sum total of physical realities still remains the framework.

Confidence in Men

During the Renaissance there was manifested a new confidence in human powers but the social implications of this new awareness were first fully faced in the eighteenth century by those who fought for the rights of men. These leaders felt confidence in what all men could do if given freedom. They had a profound belief in reason, a deep distrust of all tyrannies which control men's minds.

These men lived in a world where political, economic,

and religious power was in the hands of a few. They lived
in a time when the dead hand of tradition was strong and
that tradition backed by deeply entrenched interests.
Classical scholars and priesthoods encouraged respect for
divine revelation and discouraged self-reliance. Men were
told to accept rather than to investigate and to question.

Through the centuries religious leaders had taught that
there were laws beyond the reach of reason and that one
should follow obediently those who knew and interpreted
such laws. They taught that men should concentrate on
reaching the next world rather than center thoughts and
actions on this one.

We see here two opposing moods: the one for self-deter-
mination; the other against it. As John Herman Randall, Jr., has said, history is

. . . an alternation of two moods . . . there is the mood of
supernaturalism . . . a mood of dependence and self-abnega-
tion, a bitter realization of frustration and failure, in which
man's confidence oozes to nothingness and he feels himself
the plaything of forces which he cannot pretend to com-
prehend.

And there is the humanistic hope " involving the triumphant apotheosis of man, the creator and builder."

The eighteenth century democrats, Rousseau and Vol-
taire, believed in men's right to liberty. They felt that
only where men are free are they able to become all they
might be. Thomas Paine and Thomas Jefferson were opposed to all governments, institutions, laws, and customs
which restrained the free use of men's minds, which imposed arbitrary, unnecessary authority on how men shall
think and act.

Thomas Jefferson wrote:

I am not an advocate for frequent changes in laws and con-stitutions. But laws and institutions must go hand and hand with the progress of the human mind. As that becomes more developed, more enlightened, as new discoveries are made, new truths discovered and manners and opinions change . . . institutions must advance also to keep pace with the times. We might as well require a man to wear still the coat which fitted him when a boy as civilized society to remain ever under the regimen of their barbarous ancestors.

Men Are Equal

We are indebted in large measure to the eighteenth century democrats not only for their concept of political freedom but for the idea of political equality. Not only is there intrinsic value in each of us, but there is a basic human equality among us.

Political and religious leaders traditionally supported the theory of divine right and the notion that some indi-viduals were inherently superior to others. Some fellows with an independent turn of mind — ornery nonconform-ists who were perpetually getting into trouble — looked at all the kings, dukes, bishops, and priests and whispered the simple questions: What, if anything, makes them supe-rior? What indispensable purpose do they serve?

Mutual Aid

For centuries many religions have advanced the idea that all men are brothers and therefore should help one another. This notion, however, has fared but poorly and still is bravely struggling for survival in a largely callous world. The difficulty lies, perhaps, in that humans have been told merely that it is our duty to feel as brothers. We have been given no satisfactory reasons.

There are many reasons why the modern humanist is

convinced of the value of cooperation. In the first place, concentration of interest in the present, in this life on earth, has acted as a dynamo generating the idea that existence should be tolerable for everyone. If this is the only life we can be sure of, let us make it a worthy one.

During the last hundred years, furthermore, the humanist knows that scientists have made clear how cooperation is, in a very real sense, important to survival on many levels of life. Kropotkin pointed out how crucial to human and animal survival is the exercise of mutual aid. Patten, the paleontologist, found in cooperation the grand strategy of evolution. According to Bernard's zoological researches, the development of higher forms of life was made possible by the progressive cooperation of cells.

Things Evolve

Many early Greeks did not believe that the world had been created as of a particular date by a deity. They felt that somehow this universe with its wealth of living things had evolved from some simpler material. Certain nineteenth century scientists had come to this view but not until the publication of Darwin's *The Origin of Species* were average men and women faced with the idea of evolution.

In the first shock of this discovery most felt that a common ancestry with animals lowered the human race to a level with them. There were others, however, who sensed that in the idea of evolution there lay cause for special encouragement. While other living things must adapt themselves to nature, must change their own forms, men on account of their special gifts are able to adapt nature to themselves. The idea that men can turn the process of

evolution to their own advantage to further their own
highest good, and to recreate the world and themselves, is
at the very center of present-day humanism.

During the nineteenth century a few thinkers suggested
that moral laws have not come to us through revelation.
Herbert Spencer's strong voice announced that these are
the results of men's experiences in living with one another
and are not the precepts of any supreme being. Here we
find emphasis on the evolutionary aspect of morality.
This too contributes to our philosophy.

Experience Is Our Guide

Gradually men have learned to test the truth of their notions by experience. Within recent centuries this practical good sense has developed into the scientific method, a
method which has served the interests of mankind more
successfully, more humanely, and therefore in a sense more
spiritually, than any other. Within the past century some
of the implications of this method have become widely
known and appreciated. Most citizens of the technically
advanced countries have at least a vague faith in the practical results of scientific method. However, there have
never been many who perceived how much value there
was in using this method in one's own daily life, or in the
building of a living philosophy. Those who were able to
see it as a major tool in their total adjustment of life have
been, to that extent, in the humanist tradition.

And So — Humanism

By the twentieth century, scientists, impelled by their
own kind of interest in the world around them had been
carrying on a quiet revolution. They had built up for us

an entirely different picture of the universe — and of our place in it — from that which had been accepted in the Middle Ages.

The established religions — Christianity, Mohammedanism, Judaism, and to some extent Buddhism and Hinduism — had been built around a static picture. The new picture is so different that many have been repelled or have not been able to bring themselves to accept it. It was the impact of this new knowledge, however, which brought about the transformation of humanism into a relatively clear-cut body of ideas and into an organized movement. Humanism developed as scattered individuals and small groups realized that they had a common bond in their thorough, ungrudging acceptance of this new knowledge and its implications for men's lives.

Let us consider certain of the changes brought about in scientific knowledge during the past few centuries.

The earth, this globe of ours, once proud center of the divine handiwork, has lost considerably in geographical importance. Even our sun, itself several hundred thousand times the size of the earth, is found to be but an average-sized star on the edge of a nebula of perhaps 30 billion other stars. Beyond there are even other nebulae!

The earth, once thought to have been planned and created about 4000 B.C., is now known to have a far longer history. While it is uncertain how many millions of years ago the earth came into being, it has reached its present condition through gradual change and is still in process of evolution.

And man, once center, master, and darling of the universe for whom all else was created, has had to take a more humble position. Men appear to have evolved from lower forms of life and to differ from these less than had been supposed. Moreover, the findings of science reveal that each of us is an inseparable unity of body and personality, of mind and emotions. The soul, long thought to be man's unique possession, has evaporated into nothingness.

When the impact of this new picture was felt, the implications seemed staggering. How could people accept the new view of man and his universe? We had lost our security, our importance, we who had been the favorite sons of the creator! We who were made for a special destiny! Some even feared that our most precious human goals, purposes, ideals, lost importance in this new world.

But these implications did not stagger the humanists of thirty years ago. They had a solid faith in man. To them men needed no privileged position in the scheme of things. Having a genuine respect for, and interest in, human purposes and human ideals for their own sakes, they were not upset to find that these are not linked up with any great purposes of the universe as a whole.

Far from shrinking from the implications of biology, anthropology, astronomy, psychology, paleontology, and physiology, they made them the basis of their thinking. They built up from them the philosophy and religion of humanism.

The sociologist Frank H. Hankins regards humanism as a logical step in the human venture:

Sociological and historical researchers have shown that the essential core of religion is devotion to those social values which bind men together in cooperative effort for group preservation and mutual welfare; and that these values are discovered through human experiences. Among those discovered in recent times are devotion to truth as exemplified in the scientific mentality, the dignity of individual man, and the ideals of democracy. Humanism thus becomes the next logical step in religious evolution; it is the heir and creative fulfillment of the Renaissance, the Reformation, and the democratic revolutions.

CHAPTER THREE

Some Basic Beliefs

The Fundamental Premise

Basic to humanism is a particular approach to the world about us — to the physical and psychological environments. This approach or method is considered more important than any conclusions reached by using it. For knowledge is continually increasing. Conclusions about many things in this world have to change as knowledge grows. It is necessary to remain open-minded and often to suspend judgment. When we form a conclusion it is important that we do not force it upon other people. Whereas in most other religions and in some philosophies certain matters have been laid down, accepted on faith and held to be true for all time, this is not true in humanism. We hold in high regard the scientific method — the constant search for information and the willingness to change opinions as facts warrant. Except when he is talking of ethical values the humanist makes few assertions.

To clarify further the difference between the method of which we speak and the one used by those who accept on faith, Frances R. Dewing has written, in a letter to the authors:

One of the essential things about scientific method is an open mind, critical only of the quality of the evidence, and a

readiness to accept any conclusions. With this goes an eager-
ness to find the principles that can be used to give us successful dealings with our objective experiences. These principles
as long as they work are what we call truth.

Contrasted with this basis for truth which assumes dependence on reasoning power there is truth by authority — personal, organizational or "by the book."

This cleavage of method is a more fundamental cleavage
than cleavage according to items of conclusions, especially as
by our method any conclusion is conceivably possible. The
only negative allowable is the denial of the right of any other
person to assert a statement without showing reasons — especially to assert truth for others dogmatically.

In some ways we wish we could end the manuscript at
this point. That might leave dissatisfaction, however, as
more questions than ever may have been raised and left
unanswered.

Humanists generally hold views on mind, heaven, immortality, essences, and the ideal, which are hard for anti-
naturalists and Christians to understand. Some of these
concepts will be discussed later on, but here we wish to
point out that they are not the heart of the fourth faith.
In fact, ideas of sin, the ideal, immortality, and deity are
considered rather unimportant and are seldom discussed.

Points of General Agreement

How we believe is more important than what we believe.
Because we use the scientific method we recognize that
even our most central beliefs may have to change in the
light of further evidence.

It would be strange if thoughtful and independent
people did not have differences of opinion as to what are
the most significant ideas in their common philosophy. It
would be strange if there were no real disagreements as

to implications and emphases. The fourth faith, many-faceted, humane, experimental, has room within it for many varieties of opinion.

On some points, however, there is general agreement. Let us consider certain significant ones:

(1) Men are, in every respect, a part of nature. They are a natural product of the evolutionary process.

(2) Men, like all other living things, must rely upon themselves, upon one another, and upon nature. There is no evidence that they receive support or guidance from any immaterial power with whom they are presumed to commune.

(3) Men are able to meet the challenge of life in constantly more satisfying ways provided they are able to make full use of their capacities.

(4) The spiritual meaning of life is that which we give to it. Happiness and self-fulfillment for oneself and others are richly sufficient life goals.

(5) Moral codes are made by men. Values and ideals grow out of human experience.

(6) The supreme value is the individual human being. Each person, of whatever race or condition, is of equal worth. Laws, governments and other institutions exist for the service of men, and are justifiable only as they contribute to human well-being.

Because he believes in the capabilities of men to solve their problems, because he has confidence in the scientific method, in experience, in knowledge, and in the natural creative processes of the universe, the humanist feels that mankind can successfully continue to make better todays and build toward a better tomorrow.

CHAPTER FOUR

Answers to Some Common Questions

Are Humanists Agnostics?

Most humanists are agnostics although some are atheists. But not all agnostics and atheists are humanists.

Most humanists are agnostics for they neither affirm nor categorically deny the existence of God. They do not have what James H. Leuba called " a God to whom one may pray in the expectation of receiving an answer." Professor Leuba added, " By ' answer ' I mean more than the subjective, psychological effect of prayer." They find no evidence in the universe of any non-human personality which is concerned for the welfare of men. And therefore the question of the existence of a non-human personality is an open one. They feel that where it is perhaps impossible to know, or where we do not know definitely, it is best not to be dogmatic in either direction.

They recognize that God is thought of in a wide variety of ways. The term God is applied by some people to nature, by others to love, by others to goodness in men, and by still others to the grand design — the way things work in the universe. A humanist does not reject impersonal ideas of God, but he suggests that there are better ways of expressing these aspects of nature.

Although humanists have either an agnostic or atheistic point of view, it does not follow that all agnostics and atheists could be described as humanists. Agnosticism or atheism is a relatively unimportant part of humanist religion and philosophy. Many humanists dislike the labels of atheism and agnosticism on account of their possible negative implication. What they do not believe in counts relatively little for them; it is what they do believe in and how and why they believe this that makes them humanists.

Thomas Huxley, great champion of evolution, was the first to call himself an agnostic. He was among the first to express forcefully the idea that since we cannot know definitely about such matters as God and immortality we should base our thinking and behavior on that which we can know, such as life on earth, human need.

Harold R. Rafton, founder and president of the Humanist Fellowship of Boston, when asked, " Do you believe in a supreme being? " replied, " Emphatically yes, and that supreme being is man." Humanists are careful, however, to point out that this does not mean prideful self-worship of man by man, because humanists do not worship in the traditional sense. To be sure, the fulfilment of human life is their highest value and their goal. But they realize that this fulfilment is dependent upon men's relationship with nature as a whole. They know that nature and its laws very largely set the course and determine the goals men must seek to be fully men. Their needs, their hopes are developed in interaction with nature.

How Do Humanists Use the Bible?

Humanists find inspiration in the scriptures of Buddhism, Confucianism, Mohammedanism, Christianity, and other religions. Many humanists are students of the

Bible, and hold it in high regard. The story of the historical progression of the people in Asia Minor from belief in a tribal god to belief in a world God serves as great inspiration. The Bible, however, is not regarded as a final authority in matters of belief and morals.

Why Do Humanists Respect Jesus?

Most of them think of Jesus as a great if not the greatest ethical leader who has ever lived. To the work of the previous Jewish prophets he added a special insistence on the place of love, kindness, and forgiveness in human life. Humanists do not attribute divinity to him but find inspiration in his life and teachings. They believe that the way of life taught by Jesus has been obscured by creeds and rituals and that fundamentally his teachings were concerned with human relations and with the daily practice of the social virtues.

What Is the Humanist Basis for Morality?

It is found in the study of nature and man. Actions are evaluated in terms of their consequences.

The humanist usually looks with favor on the ethical codes of the traditional religions, but points out that in different cultures there are wide differences of opinion as to what is moral.

Some traditional religions are chiefly interested in establishing right relations with God. Humanism is concerned that through intelligent cooperation men live a good life and lessen poverty, war, disease, and prejudice. The welfare of each of us is dependent on the welfare of all. Men do not have to believe the same things but they need to recognize their common humanity and the common human aspects of their beliefs.

What Do Humanists Think about the Soul?

We are constantly learning new facts from scientists about the interrelationships of mind and body. More is ever being revealed as to how wonderfully sensitive and intricate the human nervous system is. It is becoming more and more unnecessary to explain our best thought and feeling as the result of an inner light. At this time there just does not seem to be any evidence of, or any need for, an immaterial soul.

In the works of Robert G. Ingersoll, brilliant agnostic of a half-century ago, can be found a general survey of the areas wherein traditional religious concepts no longer fit the world as men are coming to know it through study and investigation.

What Do Humanists Think about Immortality?

Immortality implies the existence of a soul, a soul which can be separated from the body. We know of no humanists who believe in a dualism of soul and body.

Edwin H. Wilson has said:

The Humanist lives as if this world were all and enough. He is not otherworldly. He holds that the time spent on the contemplation of a possible after-life is time wasted. He fears no hell and seeks no heaven, save that which he and other men create on earth. He willingly accepts the world that exists on this side of the grave as the place for moral struggle and creative living. He seeks the life abundant for his neighbor as for himself. He is content to live one world at a time and let the next life — if such there may be — take care of itself. He need not deny immortality; he simply is not interested. His interests are here.

Humanists do believe most thoroughly, however, in the kind of immortality which flows from the effects of actions, effects which often continue long after we have perished.

Was Our Country Founded on the Belief in God?

No. Lyman Hinckley has said:

Thomas Paine was the leading author, Thomas Jefferson the leading statesman, Washington the leading soldier, and Franklin the leading diplomat in the founding of our nation. Every one of them was a freethinker — in Christian terms, an infidel.

Although one might object that these men were perhaps deists rather than freethinkers, it is well to remember that at the time they lived deists were considered little different from those without any belief. We do know that these particular early Americans were not interested in identifying the government of the new country with a religious concept of any kind.

At the Constitutional Convention it was voted after some discussion that the word God would not have a place in the Constitution. George Washington while president signed in the name of the United States this statement: " The Government of the United States is not in any sense founded on the Christian religion." Our country has become strong partly through the foresight of our founding fathers.

It is discouraging to see a man such as Congressman Rabaut of Michigan try to change the pledge of allegiance to the flag by proposing to insert after " one nation " the phrase " under God." As Elmer Davis in the August 1953 issue of *Harper's* points out, there is no historical evidence that only a believer in a theological religion can have faith in freedom, in self-government, in democracy.

Do Humanists Go to Church?

Some do and some do not. Wherever there is a liberal church congregation it is likely to include one or more professed humanists. Among organized religious groups one is most likely to find humanists in Ethical Culture societies, in Unitarian, Universalist, Episcopal, and Congregational churches. There are also many in liberal Jewish and Quaker congregations.

Meetings of humanist groups are not considered church meetings. Some of these groups are, however, very little different from liberal religious organizations.

Do Humanists Have Ministers?

There is no officially organized humanist ministerial group. Churches which are primarily humanist, although not so named, have ministers belonging to some denomination — often Unitarian or Universalist. Executive secretaries, leaders, or counselors are used by various humanist groups. None of these coordinators function in the leader-follower relationship. Some counselors perform marriages and conduct funeral services, but authorization to do this depends upon complying with regulations of various states. Alfred E. Smith, as counselor of the Humanist Fellowship of Boston, represents a new type of religious leadership emerging in the movement.

Do Humanists Oppose Ceremonies and Rituals?

No. Ritual and symbolism help some persons to feel more deeply. For them these things make philosophy and belief more vivid and provide emotional and esthetic satisfactions.

Humanists, however, have tended to shy away from symbols for they have noticed how often in the past these have become fixed forms and more meaningful than the things which they originally represented. They feel that symbols should not be mistaken for that which they symbolize. They are saddened to watch them acquire a meaning of their own and lose their significance as human expressions of work, growth, abundance, family, death, life, fertility, and reverence before the unity of nature.

The beauty provided by religious symbolism and ritual has been largely lacking in humanist meetings. Among the exceptions are the services at the Charles Street Universalist Meetinghouse in Boston where Kenneth L. Patton and his congregation use religious symbols and creative rituals on a humanist basis.

Is Humanism Less Complete Than Other Religions?

No. Although lacking the rigid, fixed scriptures of an alleged revelation, the sources of inspiration, written or otherwise, which humanists use are very wide. This faith draws on all the living poetry and literature that expresses joy and hope. It cultivates the awareness of beauty and the love of man, truth and life. These are dynamic, ever-growing sources of feeling. Infused with these sources of inspiration humanism offers a complete and satisfying philosophy. It not only gives comfort and provides inspiration but it helps individuals to maintain personal well-being and to face and solve the problems of daily living.

Do Humanists Claim Absolute Certainty?

No. Dogmas are avoided. As Malcolm H. Bissell, educator and a vice-president of the American Humanist Association, has said:

For the tragedy of mankind has not been written by the searchers for the final answer, but by those who have found it. No man ever hated his brother for doubting what he himself could still question. No Columbus who *knows* what lies beyond the horizon ventures forth to find a new world. The fruitless battle of the sects has long since told its bitter and bloody tale. A thousand centuries of fears and forebodings, of priests and prayers and persecutions, have brought us only to the inscrutable stars and the silent mountains. The gods have not spoken; we ourselves must design the good society of which we dream.

Is the Humanist Faith a Satisfying One?

Growing numbers of people are finding it so. There is comfort in discovering oneself to be in a vital relationship with nature and with one's fellows. There is a sense of well-being which comes from cooperating with others for the common good, in recognizing all men as brothers — whether or not they differ in their worship rituals. The fourth faith is in harmony with the growing knowledge of the universe and its inhabitants. As a dynamic, developing point of view it sustains as well as stimulates. It challenges us to live according to the highest ideals of the human race.

Has Humanism Sacrificed All Sense of Assurance?

For some people the revealed certainty of the traditional religions has no counterpart in the humanist faith. Others feel differently.

If humanists are without a dependable fatherly being who will protect them against nature, they realize that in another sense nature itself is dependable. As men study their environment, it becomes more and more predictable and less and less frightening. As men understand and co-operate with nature they flourish. Ours is the assurance that no event, no experience, is necessarily mysterious. There is a basic sort of order and explanation, if we could but find it, for all the things that happen to us and around us.

How satisfying it has been to countless people to know that the universe as a whole, and we as individuals, have come into existence " according to nature's law."

Humanism is built on the knowledge and method of science so the humanist does not have to fear for his faith or be forever on the defensive against advancing truth. It gives therefore an assurance and security not available to those whose religion is ever in retreat before the growth of knowledge.

Do Humanists Believe the Fourth Faith Unites People?

Yes. The ethical codes of the great religions are very much alike, although there the similarity sometimes ends. Humanism is free from divisive doctrines about the unknown, free from rituals and ceremonies and liturgical regulations which so often separate people and set them apart from each other. There is no damnation, no purgatory, no heaven, no mystical realms or essences. Humanism is concerned with life on this wonderful earth of ours. The historical theologies vary, as do the ways in which men worship, but the essence of these religions — the teaching as to the way men should behave — is very much alike in all. In humanism this good moral life is justified in terms of our having proper relationships with nature and with one another. Humanists are united by their devotion to the scientific spirit and democratic faith.

Do Many People Call Themselves Humanists?

It was unusual until a few years ago for anyone who was not very successful, and lacked ability to stand up against religious prejudice and possible occupational discrimination, to admit that he was a humanist. This is changing rapidly. More and more people are becoming tired of masquerading as Protestants, Catholics, and Jews, or of assuming they are entirely without religious feeling. It is a growing practice to write " humanist " rather than " none " when questionnaires ask for one's religion.

Is the Humanist Movement Organized?

Only to a limited extent. Humanist leaders have tended to lean over backward in their concern that the fourth faith acquire none of the characteristics of a cult or a traditional religion. The American Humanist Association, with headquarters at Yellow Springs, Ohio, is the leading humanist organization in this country. It does vital educational work and is indispensable to the growth of the movement. There are more than forty groups which are affiliated with the A. H. A. in some manner or other. There are chapters, there are independent humanist fellowships, and there are study groups. In the Pacific Coast states John Danz has done much toward building several independent societies. Since the recent death of its remarkable leader C. G. Patterson, the Institute of Human Fellowship whose world headquarters was in Portland, Oregon, has merged with the A. H. A.

The primary work of the Association is in meeting the

desires and needs of individuals scattered throughout the country. Some of the larger liberal churches which have humanists among their members receive the literature of the Association, and keep in close contact with it for help in programming and many other ways. A significant number of ministers and liberal rabbis are members. The Association endeavors to assist these individuals and groups in any way it can.

Occasionally there are regional conferences in different sections of the country. Here for two or three days people meet and exchange viewpoints, gain knowledge, and feel the satisfaction of talking with others interested in ideas and in new ways of helping men adjust to their world.

The American Humanist Association has a Board of Directors and officers. There is a paid staff and there are volunteer part-time workers.

Do Humanists Expect Other Churches to Close Their Doors?

No. They merely believe that the established churches will continue to become more humanistic. They point with pleasure to the growing concern about social conditions within leading churches throughout the world. They note the liberalizing influences at work within Jewish and Protestant groups in America and the changing attitude of many Catholics.

Humanists question the idea that religious needs must be met in certain ways and in those ways only.

Do Humanists Believe Their Movement Will Grow?

Yes. They believe it is only a matter of time until the fourth faith will affect millions of lives everywhere. They point to its rapid growth within the past three years. And they believe that viewpoint is in the mainstream of human advance.

A few humanists have almost missionary zeal. They are among those who may have recalled the words of Buddha, " The world is undone, quite undone, when the heart of the truth seeker inclines to rest quiet, rather than proclaim his doctrine."

Many Unitarian, Universalist, and other liberal churches are tending ever more toward the humanist position. In other countries millions of people are ready to take up this new religion of humanity.

Ten years ago active interest in humanism was largely confined to men and women who were making substantial contributions to the arts, sciences, and philosophy. Less than ten years ago it was estimated that a third of the members of the American Humanist Association were included in " Who's Who in America," or " Who's Who in Science." Today there is a higher percentage of less eminent though thoughtful people. A number of men and women in their twenties and thirties are vigorously spreading knowledge of the fourth faith. For them it is a glorious adventure in personal understanding and development. These include such energetic humanists as Taylor Rhodes, Paul Schwenneker, James V. Grasso, Warren Allen Smith, William F. Lennon, Jr., Robert Quest, William H. Stalnaker, Howard Cox, Jean Jackson Kirschbaum, Robert Kelso, Abraham Pollock, William James Hall, Melvin W. Berg, and Harold Rightmyer.

CHAPTER FIVE

How Humanism Meets Personal Needs

Three Basic Needs

Philosophy and religion serve people in various ways. For some individuals these meet many of their psychological needs, for others very few. But it can be agreed that in almost all instances philosophy and religion offer at least to some extent a means of comfort and self-respect, a source of ethical standards, and a wellspring of inspiration, and that by so doing they fulfill fundamental needs.

Most people would concede that the older religions offer these satisfactions. How do the ideas which are at the core of the fourth faith give comfort, give ethical standards, give inspiration?

Mental and Emotional Security

Religions in the past have given us a very comfortable position in the universe. We had the reassurance of knowing that we were in contact with a power beyond nature which gave the human race love and protection. Like those who sponsored the appeal for funds after the 1953 tornado in Worcester, Massachusetts, by saying, " Remember, God spared you," we knew that the Almighty had us constantly in mind.

Today we still need some kind of basic reassurance about our relationship to the world in order to know that we have a place, that we are accepted. Most of the time our friends, our family, our work, give us some sense of belonging. However, for many of us there are times when these are not enough, when we have to turn elsewhere for security. Then, perhaps feeling lonely and unwanted, we draw renewed courage and comfort from a reassuring picture of ourselves in relation to God, or to a larger whole — the universe, the world, or humankind.

How can humanism give this kind of picture? How can a philosophy which questions whether there is any unique concern for the human race either in nature or beyond it give religious and philosophical reassurance?

Humanism teaches first that there is an intrinsic, in-alienable value in all human beings. This is not a value that has been given us by a deity or that we hold only because we have earned it. It is our birthright. We can have a mystical and poignant depth of feeling about this. At the very heart of our philosophy is a warmly genuine sense of the value in every man, whatever his ability, however he is circumstanced.

This can be the foundation for an invulnerable sense of self-respect. The feeling of security that comes to one who has this kind of self-respect enables him to withstand the incidence of misfortune, and of disgrace. It even stands firm against those savage attacks that we sometimes level at ourselves. This kind of feeling about oneself is still appropriate no matter into what shameful mess one has become involved.

Secondly, humanism encourages us to feel that no matter who we are we have untapped abilities, unknown potentialities, and more strength, inventiveness, and genius for survival and progress than we know. We are to look for strength not outside ourselves but within. Erich Fromm, in his book *Psychoanalysis and Religion*, speaks of the value of having a faith in the power within ourselves to meet life with courage. Some philosophies and religions stress how weak, how evil, and how foolish we are by nature. Although they offer a way of overcoming this lack of strength, virtue, and wisdom, they first impress on us our deficiencies. How much better it is to emphasize hope and self-confidence. How much better to believe that we must and can take care of ourselves.

Thirdly, it teaches us to look for courage, for comfort, to one another, our fellow humans, of whom there are some two and a quarter billion. A humanist is like the soldier who feels an exhilarating interdependence with his comrades when faced with a common danger. We all have experienced the pleasantness of a sense of closeness with a group of strangers when we suffered some minor mishap together, for instance the breakdown of a subway train between stops. Why can not this satisfying sense of solidarity be called up in all of us by the realization that humankind can expect no special dispensation from the universe? Is it not stimulating and comforting to acknowledge our dependence on one another?

Finally, for many humanists their deepest sense of security comes from feeling themselves an integral part of nature. A. Eustace Haydon has expressed this beautifully:

The humanist has a feeling of perfect at-homeness in the universe. He is conscious of himself as an earth child. There is a mystic glow in this sense of belonging. Memories of his long ancestry still ring in muscle and nerve, in brain and germ cell. Rooted in millions of years of planetary history, he has a secure feeling of being at home, and a consciousness of pride and dignity as a bearer of the heritage of the ages and a growing creative center of cosmic life.

This sense of belonging comes to those who realize that we are in every respect a part of nature — a nature far larger, far older, than ourselves.

All through history men have been eager to have a close relationship with the nonhuman world about them. Humanism makes this relationship obvious and logical. We feel a myriad of ties with other living creatures. We feel an enriching expansion of sympathy and interest. Living things are fellow experiencers of life, knowing fears of rejection and injury, the satisfactions of acceptance, warm sun, good food. We do not claim special privileges and are ready to face, with other living creatures, the full force of the joys and tragedies of life and death.

In years past many of nature's processes were considered entirely unpredictable and strange. The gods served as special protection against a nature often cruelly hostile. Now that we are learning through science the chains of cause and effect underlying many of these events, they tend to seem less mysterious, less frightening. The idea that there is a kind of basic coherence behind occurrences gives a measure of security. As Ruth T. Abbott often says, there is a strong, deep certainty in nature's laws.

In these several ways humanism gives a sense of security. Certain privileges have been given up but in their place we have gained self-reliance and a closer bond with our fellow humans and with the universe.

Ethical Standards

A second need felt by humans is for a standard of behavior, for ethics. Behind many of the moral codes of the past has been the pressure, the force, of eternal laws, eternal rewards and punishments. How does humanism build its ethics and standards of behavior, how does it enforce them?

Ethics in the humanist view is largely the responsibility we have for the happiness of others. There are no inflexible rules in personal ethics, for what will be ethical in one situation will not necessarily be so in another. The question of right and wrong is a very practical one. How will behavior affect the well-being of others at a particular time and place?

Our precious social virtues cannot be pressed into the character of individuals by precepts or by authority. We should act honestly, justly, considerately because we feel that this is the natural, the necessary way to behave.

A sturdy basis for ethical behavior is self-respect. The humanist knows that if he is of value, so are others; if he has a right to happiness, self-fulfilment, so have others. And self-respect develops when an individual achieves personal maturity, when he understands his strengths and limitations, and recognizes the position of men and women in the scheme of things.

Dr. Rudolf Dreikurs, a psychiatrist and a vice-president of the American Humanist Association, has expressed this thought in two of his " Ten Premises for a Humanist Philosophy of Life." He says:

Man's greatest obstacle to full social participation and co-operation is an underestimation of his own strength and value. . . . Man's greatest evil is fear. Courage and belief in his own ability are the basis for all his virtues. Through his realization of his own value he can feel belonging to others, and be interested in others.

There are deep in this philosophy many ideas which encourage one to feel thus connected with, and interested in, other people.

Humanists gain a bond with others when they recognize that men must and can help one another in common problems, against common obstacles.

The fourth faith also provides us the strongest possible motive for kindliness and consideration, for justice and honesty. If we believe there will be no second chance in a future life to make up to family, friends, and acquaintances for the difficulties and unhappiness which we cause them, and if we believe there is no future of bliss for them but that this life we share is all they will ever know, it becomes crucial that we do what we can to make this existence a happy one.

We are not quick to condemn the simpler, more elementary enjoyments. We do not think of these as unimportant or debased. We do not suggest that the pleasures from, say eating a Maine lobster dinner, or of sunning on the beach, are not worth much. Happiness is a great good and we should accept it where and when it is offered to us.

Because we do not make the distinction between an admirable soul and a less admirable body, we do not separate ourselves into two parts. One part of ourselves is not respected while another part is scorned. We seek the best development of the whole personality. We refuse to set up fierce battles between impulse and conscience and therefore there is no endless inner struggle between good and evil. The normal sex drive, for instance, is not thought of as evil in itself. Like all basic human needs it is not intrinsically wrong but does harm when not directed toward socially useful goals.

Accounts given by anthropologists of ethics in regions as varied as Samoa, Togoland, and England are more than merely entertaining. They show that what is considered right behavior with respect to one's neighbor or one's sister-in-law is different in various parts of the world. Our standards of behavior have grown up, slowly and painfully, from the particular experiences of the group into which we happen to be born.

Aubrey Menen, writing in the July 4, 1953, issue of *The New Yorker,* tells us that until very recently any married woman in Malabar who wore clothes above her waist was considered to be aiming at adultery. It was unthinkable for a cultured adult to sit eating with another, for this would require putting food into the mouth, chewing, and swallowing in public. As for sitting in one's own dirty bath water — never!

Yet societies have traditionally felt the need not only for codes of behavior but for some kind of superhuman, eternal justification for them. There has been widespread belief that what is right and what is wrong must be eternally right and wrong and right and wrong for all. It has often been thought that unless people believe this they will think lightly of codes and standards.

However, the realization that ethics are built up by men for the use of men is in no respect dangerous. Isn't there something appealingly practical and wholesome in the notion that good behavior is that which leads to human welfare? This point of view seems the best kind of justification of and encouragement to honesty and unselfishness.

When a code of behavior is thought to be handed down from a greater power, one obeys from reverence or from fear. There is often the added incentive of punishment or reward. Humanists do not have these forms of persuasion. They like the ones they have — the expectation that people will want to follow those standards which have proved best for the general good, and the recognition that an individual who is mature in body, mind, heart, and spirit is eager to work for the common welfare.

And many humanists see beneath all differences in customs and codes a common denominator. They see the principle of mutual aid as a law of survival.

This, then, is humanist ethics.

Inspiration

We need more than ethics, more than comfort, from a philosophy or religion. We need inspiration. We need to express the upreaching and inspiring impulse in human life. We hunger for beauty.

Inspired by an idea or by a symphony of sensory impressions we feel alive. Our senses dance, our spirits soar. The crusts of routine and monotony are cracked. The concerns of everyday life are seen in a new perspective, seen in terms of what is supremely worthwhile. Life takes on a new meaning. A thoroughly inspirational idea also leads to some kind of purposeful behavior. One is not only inspired but inspired to act in an unaccustomed direction or to be a different kind of person.

There is a deeply inspirational quality in humanism. Many are drawn to the fourth faith because it has power to inspire them as nothing else does.

This may seem to be a paradox. How, one could ask,

can a point of view inspire which questions whether there
is any absolute and preordained meaning to human existence? How can a philosophy inspire which doubts that
man has a role to play in a moral drama transcending
life and death?

Yet it is these very ideas which seem deeply, obviously
inspirational to humanists. Alfred E. Smith, in a lecture
to the Humanist Fellowship of Boston, expressed this
feeling:

When you have arrived at the humanist perspective of life,
fully realizing that in all the universe there is no concern for
man excepting man's concern for himself, no meaning to life
except the meaning which man himself gives to life, no reason
or excuse for existence except the possibility that man can
make existence worth while — when you have that perspective,
that realization, then there comes to you an urgency to do
everything you can to make your life more meaningful, more
joyous, more worthwhile.

Many years ago John Dietrich put this idea into other
words for his Minneapolis congregation:

Although the universe cares not about our ideals and our
morality, we must care for them. All the virtues and all the
values, all there is of goodness and justice, kindliness and cour-
tesy is of our own creation and we must sustain them, or
otherwise they will go out of existence.

And further,

Against the terrifying background of an uncaring universe,
we may each set a triumphant soul that has faced facts without dismay, and knowing good and evil, chosen good.

Many humanists would maintain that here too sharp
a line has been drawn between men and the rest of nature.
They would remind us that our aspirations and our ideals
are related to those larger laws that govern all natural

things. They might point out that any meaning to life which a man may discover satisfies him just because it is in harmony with the laws of nature. But this is a matter of emphasis, of difference in response. For some of us it is the idea of our human isolation and independence which seems particularly meaningful; for others, it is the idea of our interdependence with the nonhuman world. What unites humanists is the conviction that it is to ourselves we must look if we wish to find a master plan by which to shape and give direction to our lives. There is no realm, no force, no personality beyond nature which is the source of meaning and value or which leads us and directs us. Nor is there a special group of religious or philosophical leaders in control of the keys to human virtue and human happiness. We must find them for ourselves.

The reason, of course, why this conviction inspires rather than discourages is confidence that we can do this. The humanist sees a worthwhile job to be done and he believes that he can do it. Little wonder he feels inspired. He has been given a challenge.

For further inspiration he turns to those fundamental ideas which have given him comfort, security, and self-respect.

His sense of unity with all mankind has at times a mystical quality. It can also be exhilarating. The well-loved phrase, "All men are brothers," has a particular force, a special ring. The humanist is keenly aware of the plight of *homo sapiens,* a species which although a part of nature has risen through agelong evolution to a position different from and set apart from other species. A. Eustace Haydon describes humankind as " the only thinking things in all the vastness of time and space. Alone here for a moment between birth and death, a spectacle so pitiful, so tragic and so grand." It is against this stark picture of man's isolated place in the world, of his sensitivities, his powers, that the humanist sees all members of our human race wherever they may be — in Cairo, in Paris, or in Houston. He identifies himself with all people for he sees their problems as human problems. He is completely and irrevocably committed to the human adventure.

The humanist is filled with wonder and admiration at the creature that is man, at his capacity for accomplishment, for sacrifice, at the intricacy and precision of that nervous system which has made it possible for him to stand where he does today in nature's hierarchy. He is convinced that if we use to an ever greater extent our unique capacities for discovery and for cooperation the future of our race will be a brilliant and a happy one.

Most humanists are moved by the constant realization that men are children of nature in every fiber of their being, in every fleeting thought. Both exaltation and humility spring from knowing that we live out our lives within a great enveloping process far larger, far older, than ourselves. Many people feel this is the very heart of their life philosophy. Ruth T. Abbott says: " Our relatedness to the whole of nature is our strength and our source of ethics and our fire in being." Certainly if we consider man's fascinating relation to the universe, we are both lifted up and humbled, both disciplined and supported.

Where can one find more astonishing and ironic paradox, more poetry, more mystery than in this relationship? Nature tenderly provides us with the most delicate and precise of apparatus for our health and survival. It does the same for the mosquito and the tubercle bacillus. Humankind is lifted to ecstasy by sunset color on mountain peaks and is sickened with disgust by decaying flesh. Our species feels gratitude for warm sun and clean water, despair before tornadoes and burning droughts. Humanists, freed from the necessity of thinking that the natural world was created for human satisfaction or edification are able to take nature as it comes. Knowing that men are fools to expect any special consideration, we are spared the shock of disillusionment and are unencumbered by the notion that nature rewards those we call good and punishes those we call evil. We are freed from bitterness and can feel a single-minded, wholehearted joy and interest in the beautiful, the orderly, and the awesome aspects of the universe.

Yet for all our calm objectivity we happily confess a connectedness with nature so close that it is almost complete identification. Our most dramatic aesthetic and intellectual triumphs are as much the products of natural processes as the dams of beavers or the hives of bees. For us the really exciting and fascinating paradox lies in the fact that for all our efforts to be objective, we cannot set ourselves apart, for in a sense we ourselves are nature. The meaning of the word "nature" is expanded to include all those most delicate, subtle, and noble of our aspirations that hitherto men have been loath to admit as belonging to the natural world. To us — and this is perhaps the most difficult thing for the nonhumanist to understand — the effect of putting men in nature is not their debasement but the addition to nature of an exciting new dimension.

We look upon evolution of living things as one of the elemental processes in this grand integrated whole. We feel that men can now play a decisive role in this process. Man's imagination, his use of symbols, his ability to organize yesterday's experience into tomorrow's dream, set him above all other levels of life. On account of this he not only adapts himself to nature, but he is able to fashion or recreate parts of the natural world about him. Cora L. Williams in *Creative Involution* gave an inspiring picture of the human race as master of the evolutionary process. Philosophers of science have seen great hope for the future if men will awake to the possibilities of directing evolution by human knowledge, human good will.

Inspired by a sense of solidarity with his fellows, by bright confidence in the future of the human adventure, and by his relation with nature, the humanist is eager for the practical challenge with which life confronts him.

For most of us this challenge has lain chiefly in the role that we might play in the building of a better community, a finer nation, a happier world.

Increasing numbers are also thinking of what their rich and varied philosophy means in terms of personal living. When all is said and done, it is the individual and the individual's own life that matters.

Humanism teaches two things which seem at first contradictory but which actually complement and strengthen each other. It teaches us on the one hand how deeply involved we are with nature and with our fellow human beings. On the other hand it encourages us to be independent and self-reliant. We cannot play our part well and responsibly unless we are spiritually weaned. Yet we become more fully developed only through social relationships.

Erich Fromm, Rudolf Dreikurs, Harry A. Overstreet, and others have made clear how important it is for one to be free, to be independent. They show that only as one has self-respect can one have wholesome love for others, can feel concern for others, can live adequately with others in our common life.

H. J. Blackham, secretary of the International Humanist and Ethical Union, in *Living as a Humanist* describes the value of active participation in life. A humanist says "yes to life." He is ready and eager for new responsibilities, new human relationships, new experiences of every kind. He takes full part in life and at the same time full responsibility for his own past actions. On occasion it may be strenuous to say "yes to life." Blackham writes:

The use and enjoyment of what life in the world offers is not to be had by wanting, nor merely by asking, but only by intelligent, instructed and sustained effort.

An unknown Sanskrit writer expresses the daily challenge of life:

Listen to the Exhortation of the Dawn!
Look to this Day!
For it is Life, the very Life of Life.
In its brief course lie all the
Varieties and Realities of your Existence:
The Bliss of Growth,
The Glory of Action,
The Splendour of Beauty;
For Yesterday is but a Dream,
And To-morrow is only a Vision,
But To-day well lived makes

Every Yesterday a Dream of Happiness,
And every To-morrow a Vision of Hope.
Look well, therefore, to this Day!
Such is the Salutation of the Dawn.

Humanism urges us to recognize in our personal lives the importance of its fundamental method. Human progress as a whole depends on freedom to search for the truth. Individual progress also depends, in the same crucial way, on a constant search for truth about oneself. Only as one grows in self-knowledge will one become truly free. Only as one understands one's self can life offer its deeper meanings and be experienced to the full.

Rollo May has pointed out that problems of modern men and women center very often in a basic emptiness and in indifference to themselves. Alfred E. Smith has added:

Everything that a humanist is, everything that he is dedicated to, every aspect of his life, is pointed in the opposite direction. There can be no emptiness for the man or woman determined to explore and understand and affirm the meaning of life.

It is clear that humanism offers comfort and support, guidance and inspiration and a summons. In urging us to know not only the world but ourselves it offers a quest that will never end.

CHAPTER SIX

Applying Humanism to Personal Problems

The General Approach

Humanism is practical. It helps us to understand complex situations, to solve problems and to make decisions. If this were not true humanism could not be an adequate way of life. Although it provides no ready-made formulas it gives a specific point of view. This point of view makes it easier to work problems through to solution. It prevents us from creating new problems in the process of meeting old ones. This approach to difficulties is made up of two elements.

In the first place it is a certain state of mind. This is one of self-reliance and confidence. People and things act as they do from perfectly natural causes. As these are natural causes rather than occult ones there is hope of understanding and perhaps even of controlling them. Success or failure does not depend on the conjunction of Mars and Jupiter on whether it is our lucky day or on the fact that Aunt Aggie came to call. It depends on whether we can see the chains of cause and effect leading up to the present situation and on whether we act on the basis of this knowledge. This is both a disciplinary and

an encouraging philosophy. We are allowed no trans-
cendental alibis but we are freed from insoluble riddles.
We are encouraged to feel that there is usually some kind
of answer to a problem if we could but find it.

In the second place this approach involves reliance on
a certain method. There is willingness to use this method
on all problems whether routine or serious, clear-cut or
vague, practical or emotional. This procedure is the scientific method. It consists in keen observation, thorough
gathering of facts, and the careful checking of hypotheses.
It demands a mind continuously open for new knowledge
and ever reluctant to jump to conclusions.

Fixed convictions, prejudices, and dogmas are tested
against experience and the objective findings of others.
To a humanist this first step can be taken whether buy-
ing a clothes dryer or deciding what one's attitude should
be toward an alcoholic relative.

The method requires that when there is time and opportunity to gather information, as much should be col-
lected as seems practicable. On the basis of this, tempo-
rary conclusions can be drawn and tested. This course can
be followed alike in choosing a diet for quick reducing or
a candidate for mayor. Where there is no time for this,
as often in everyday life, we can at least keep our minds
open for new and better ways of meeting difficulties.
(That is, if we meet difficulties!)

Problems Involving Other People

Many of the problems of everyday life are easily resolved by coupling confidence and curiosity. We must
admit, however, that more is usually needed when there
are complex relationships with other humans.

A humanist looks at problems in social relations from a characteristic perspective. He sees them as problems in human happiness, problems in working out what will be best for the people concerned. He does not believe in taking time out to ask who is or is not right or wrong. As a practical man and as one who recognizes no hard-and-fast categories of good and evil, he is interested in workable solutions and happy relationships. To him there are not good and bad people, merely good and bad behavior and he judges behavior by its effect on others. He approaches the situation with confidence in, and liking for, the people involved. He respects the point of view of others and realizes that they have equal right with himself to their special slants. He is nondogmatic, good-humored, in a word, democratic.

A humanist has more than a broad perspective. From his kit he takes the tool of scientific method which he is as ready to use on personal as on other problems. He realizes that this tool is particularly useful when dealing with human beings for each of us is psychologically complex and subtly different. He knows that each has inherited a different make-up and that this bundle of characteristic traits has in turn been molded by very different life experiences. He understands also how important it is to recognize that people change. They may react very differently when applying for their first job than when applying for their first old-age pension check; they respond differently to a domineering father-in-law than to an attractive secretary. The humanist concludes from this that the reasons for people's behavior and changes in behavior are peculiar to each person and to each person's history. He realizes that a man often has no inkling of why he acts as he does — and that his friends often know even less about it.

Here, if ever, is a field where the facts are complex and hidden and where it is difficult to check on suppositions. But armed with his point of view the humanist will humbly be prepared to keep his mind open for new insights. He will refrain from laying down hard-and-fast rules as to how friends and relatives will or should act. He will try to understand rather than to judge.

We can easily summarize this general approach to human relations. It is only by accepting people as they are and by trying to understand them that we can live with them successfully.

Some problems involve clear-cut disagreements, impasses, where the people concerned are at cross purposes. Perhaps relatives are disagreeing as to the distribution of inherited property, or perhaps one neighbor is disputing with another the right to keep chickens in his backyard. (Let us assume that no one follows his impulse to flee!) A suitable approach to these disagreements would be a good-humored, cheerful concentration on the job of finding some kind of acceptable compromise rather than an insistence that someone is wrong and to blame. Facts would be gathered and shared. There would be great interest in finding out what was really " eating " the various people involved and why. There would be willingness to explore several possible solutions and confidence that because of the potential good will of everyone some mutual understanding could be found.

There are times when one has to make an important decision about another person. The method used by a humanist consists in bringing into focus all we know about this individual.   But it does not necessarily end with this.   Because we have faith in people, because we realize that they often mature with experience and learn from their mistakes, that past actions are the result of special circumstances, we do not make hard and inflexible judgments on the basis of past actions alone.

A Practical Example

Let us consider a hypothetical situation where this flexible point of view is put into practice.

Joanne is in her second year in a college fifty miles from her home town.   Last week she met John, a boy she had known in high school.   He was wearing the uniform of a milk company for which he now works.

Joanne hesitated when John asked her for a date.   She said she would call him in a couple of days and let him know.

In high school she had liked John intensely and had enjoyed being with him.   But John had got into a scrape just after graduation about two years ago.   Joanne never was sure what the whole story was but it included his being held by the police after a raid on a lovers' lane.   John's coupe, without the lights on, had smashed into the convertible of a prominent union leader's son.   Somehow, John had had to spend several days in jail because, it was rumored, his parents were unwilling to help him, saying he had sinned.

Joanne's parents had forbidden her to see John any more, and had told her he was a good-for-nothing.   John had had to go to work to pay for the collision damages and hadn't gone on to college.

Joanne, after this chance meeting, got to thinking

whether she should follow her desire and make the date. She tried to consider the matter in its total framework. In her reading she had come across the thought that "nothing is more certain in modern society than that there are no absolutes."

Are not laws and codes and customs as well as institutions made for humans and not the other way around? And what human good or end would be served by not associating with John?

Then Joanne thought of another principle: that we have an inherent capacity for development. We grow and change. What is true at one time may not be so at another.

John, as any other human, is neither all good nor all bad. And, after all, what is meant by good or bad as applied to a person? There is no quality of goodness or badness within people. Each person behaves in many different ways — ways which have different consequences.

Joanne frowned when she thought for a few moments of a friend whose behavior was not high-grade but who nevertheless felt in the clear because she regularly went to confession.

Joanne went to the telephone and made the date.

A few days after the date Joanne's telephone rang and her mother tearfully reported she had heard that Joanne was seen in a movie theater with John.

Joanne was tempted to shout back some accusations over the telephone but she caught herself and said that she would explain everything to her parents when she saw them at home that weekend.

This gave her additional time to think the matter out and to ponder the varying points of view concerned, in-

cluding that of her parents. She decided it would be fool-
ishness to talk with her mother about any relativity in
morals but she could discuss other phases of the situation.

When the time came, she told her mother how hard it
was on the proverbial dog which had been given a bad
name. She pointed out that, while John's behavior may
have been bad, he did have many good qualities, and that
people do change.

Because she was interested in people as individuals, and
because she had confidence in human capacities, it was
easy for her to realize that " goodness " and " badness "
are verbal abstractions, though useful verbal shorthand
for describing how we feel about the behavior of someone
else. This little story about Joanne and John also shows
that the idea of accepting people, of trying to understand
people, involves sometimes the taking of a chance. We
take the chance that people will act as we, in our friendly
confidence, expect them to.

Living with Others

Most of the time disputes or important decisions about
people are not our main problems. Our daily concern is
our adjustment to those with whom we work and live.
Often we want more than merely to get along; we want to
build rich and happy relationships. How does a humanist achieve these with his child, his wife, his mother-in-law,
his neighbor, his boss, his employee, yes, even his tele-
vision repair man?

The humanist accepts an individual as he is. Given
this person with his particular habit patterns, his particular slant on life, what is the best way of achieving a satisfactory relationship?

He would respect another's right to be different. Realizing the complexities of humankind he would attempt to understand. He would reroute his energies from irritation, boredom, or anxiety into efforts to interpret why his cousin is so irritating, his neighbor so boring, or his employees such bullies.

He realizes that you cannot bring happiness to those you love unless you accept them and understand them. He learns those things that upset, frighten, or irritate them and he endeavors to discover why. If his wife is nervous on high places he will not laugh at her, nor lecture her on how irrational and neurotic she is. He will understand that her attitude can only change slowly as its cause is learned, that the cure lies in large part in giving her the feeling of being accepted.

The humanist's acceptance is not passive. He does not see another merely as he is in his present circumstances or state of mind — of nerves, perhaps! He thinks of him as he might be, free from those tensions, hostilities, fears, which influence him to act as he does.

If the humanist gives those around him the kind of understanding which has expectation in it, he is in turn helping to change their attitudes for the better.

But it is not enough to accept and to understand the other person. We must try to accept and understand ourselves.

In any real dispute or disagreement the humanist feels the same kind of respect for himself as he has for others. He respects his own right to his personal point of view. He has little interest in brooding privately on whether he is or is not to blame for a past or present difficult situation.

He realizes that nothing is of more importance in his relationships with others than self-knowledge. Here as nowhere else is the value of the scientific method vindicated. He knows that he can discover more about himself than he can ever come to know of other people. He realizes that self-knowledge will produce improvement in his relationships more quickly than any insight he may gradually acquire about others. After an unnecessary quarrel, a reunion with an old friend spoiled by awkwardness on both sides, or after an exasperating inability to stand up for what he believes in front of others, he can ask himself: Why did I act as I did? This self-examination will be more fruitful, and will have more far-reaching effect, than any other.

Living with Oneself

Lying behind the problems of daily life there are often deeper ones, problems of hostility and fear. These are basic attitudes which are reactions to past experiences. In this case the search for self-knowledge must be carried on with more persistence and patience.

Within each of us are these fears, tensions, frustrations, and hostilities. It is as though inner demons were urging us to self-destruction. Such is the picture psychiatrists have given of humankind.

To free ourselves from these hostilities and fears we have a humanist faith which gives self-respect and security, inspiration and independence.

As one comes to be tolerant and understanding of oneself there is increasing personal maturity. Frustrations become fewer, hostilities lessen in intensity. Through the application of the scientific method one is better able to master the inner demons. Creative abilities become released. One more nearly approximates the person one might be. Deep inner problems surface and are resolved. Anxiety, boredom, and loneliness become less frequent callers. The individual becomes more of a person.

CHAPTER SEVEN

Applying Humanism to Social Problems

Humanism as a Spur to Action

Humanism gives a point of view not only valid in personal and psychological matters but in the social and economic situations of our time. It is a stimulus and a guide to making better sense out of our complex, jumbled world.

Curtis W. Reese, a former president of the American Humanist Association, has said:

Humanism is a philosophy . . . in contrast to all forms of fatalistic determinism as applied to human situations and all forms of laissez faire as applied to social situations.

Writing for the First International Congress on Humanism and Ethical Culture, he continued:

While by its very nature, scientific religion cannot be sectarian, and by its understanding of the nature and purpose of economy it cannot be partisan, yet by its role as a motivating and enlightening force it can explore and pioneer, it can judge and condemn, it can challenge and inspire. It can infuse laboratories and factories with the spirit of holiness. It can throw the mantle of sacredness over the common affairs of man, and it can make of human economy a divine adventure.

" Our supreme responsibility is the moral obligation to be intelligent," according to Oliver L. Reiser. He believes that this is the obligation to know what is going on in the world and to see insofar as we can that social change is headed in a right direction. The world is going to continue to change, and those of us sufficiently stout of heart and head can help in the grand undertaking.

If ever there was a point of view which inspires considered action, and the application of theory to practice, it is that of the fourth faith.

Consider these central ideas. We ourselves must take responsibility for making the world a better place in which to live; there is no being or power, called by whatever name, to whom we can shift this task. We have the means to improve the world through effective use of our human abilities.

Humanism badgers us by saying that we can look only to ourselves for help and then encourages us by saying that we do not need any other help. What other articles of faith are so likely to stimulate purposeful action?

The Dream

Humanists are interested in making this a better world. There is no doubt as to that. What kind of a world are they working toward?

They dream of a world in which people find outlets for their energies and opportunities to use their capacities, a world in which reasonable physical and economic needs can be satisfied, a world enriched through widespread participation in painting, dancing, music, and the other arts. Democratic method and scientific method will be more often merged for in essence they are the same — both are based on freedom to find and to weigh new courses of action, both are opposed to giving weight to arbitrary prestige, tradition. This improved society will not be a soulless, mechanistic one left to the management of so-called experts.

Most of the citizenry will be wide-awake and will take part in arriving at group discussions and in selecting capable representatives. The right to be different, to be oneself, will be respected. People will be ready to have more creative and scientific methods applied in the educational systems. Courts, hospitals, and other institutions will be more carefully planned to help those requiring their services. When psychologists and social scientists agree on ways of helping individuals and society, it will be the practice to make use of such information. As a result of this procedure, much of the present mystery shrouding the questions as to how men can be more content, maintain a higher level of personal activity and well-being, and have satisfactory human interrelationships will be dissipated.

Both amateur and professional artists will find encouragement for creative work. The money god will have retreated and there will be general appreciation of that ideal whereby free time for creative expression is valued as highly as mere pieces of silver.

Freedom for All

Whether or not one considers men as pivocs (*poor innocent victims of circumstance*) is largely a matter of temperament. Men are beset on every side with forces which crowd in on them. In the January 1, 1949, issue of the *New Yorker* that liking and respect for the individual which is at the very heart of humanism is vividly expressed:

In 1949, the individual was busy fighting to retain his status. The tide was strongly against him. He fights for the security of his person, for the freedom of his conscience, for the right to speak and the right to listen and the right not to listen when the speaking is too dull or too loud. Everywhere the individual feels the state crowding him, or the corporation crowding him, or the church crowding him, or the home crowding him. The enigma today is not the energy locked in one atom but the strength stored in a single man — the ability of this man to survive when he is always half submerged in something bigger (but not really) than he is. Here, at the end of 1948, we stretch out our mitt to this fellow.

Is it not a source for wonder that men are so magnificently resilient? Deep within them is the urge to affect circumstance, to create. The suppression of this impulse leads to personal unhappiness and dis-ease, and in a way to a blocking of the evolutionary process. There are psychological limits beyond which society and the environment should not press or crowd an individual.

Above all else, perhaps, the humanist believes in freedom; he believes that not only is it a man's right to speak and act as he chooses — within the limits of public safety — but that freedom is the means by which he can develop his human potentialities.

Behind the humanist's convictions is the faith that life can offer much contentment and be a satisfying experience for those allowed self-respect and freedom. He believes that all men are equal — equal in the sense that all men have the right to these things. For some humanists the right of each man to his individuality, the right to be different, is the essence of their philosophy.

The humanist is a profound believer in protecting the rights of all individuals, in seeing that they have equal civil liberties. Whereas there are wide differences of opinion as to the degree to which the state should regulate the lives of citizens — in such matters as regulation of private industry, labor, and price and wage controls — there is no real disagreement among them over the need of giving each citizen as much freedom as is practically possible. They feel that the individual should express himself as he chooses, join what groups he chooses, read what he chooses.

We are reminded here of what Thoreau said: " If a man does not keep pace with his companions, perhaps it is because he hears a different drummer. Let him step to the music he hears."

And remember Aldous Huxley's observation: " Among many other things, democracy is non-interfering, is leaving other people alone."

Humanists are in agreement that no strong country, not even the United States, should take advantage of its strength to dictate to a weaker nation how it should run its affairs. The Western world has no right to assume that it has been ordained in the heavens to be the leader and teacher of the Eastern world. The humanist respects all cultures as appropriate ways in which societies have built up reaction patterns to life. There is no one " necessarily better " type of culture.

Social Action

Humanism's active concern for social reforms has sometimes led to its being called applied Christianity. It is true that usually where there is a vigorous effort to effect a basic social reform, such as a court case in defense of someone's civil liberty, there is at least one recognized humanist actively involved.

But any conclusions regarding desirable social action are not as important as the quality of the method used in arriving at these conclusions. This scientific method is basic to the humanist philosophy. Before turning to see how this method might be employed by someone deeply concerned with social problems, let us consider some of the activities in which many humanists are now at work. It is only fair to mention that some of these programs and causes are not approved by all humanists.

(1) They encourage scientific research into the under-lying reasons for social tensions and personal ill-health. They encourage the widespread use of new scientific knowledge. This interest in science for humanity might be considered particularly far-reaching and characteristic.

(2) They fight for civil liberties. They believe that those, including Senator Joseph McCarthy, who would limit certain phases of our civil rights, who would spread suspicion, distrust, and dissension among ourselves, are often unaware of the harm which results from their meth-ods. Each individual of the United States, each individual of the world, has certain inalienable rights, and it is the preservation and extension of these rights for which hu-manists fight.

(3) They work to lessen racial prejudices. They con-sider the barriers which separate people to be primarily psychological. Education of many kinds is needed to com-bat the ignorance which lies behind racial hates and jeal-ousies. Where members of cultural groups appear to have objectionable traits, these usually disappear when

full cultural and economic opportunities are shared with them by the rest of society.

(4) They give full support to the United Nations and to its divisions including the United Nations Educational, Scientific, and Cultural Organization, the World Health Organization, and the Food and Agricultural Organization. The U.N. is not regarded as perfect but as having accomplished great good in keeping open avenues of communication among nations, and in keeping alive certain ideals. The strengthening of the U.N. will go a long way toward lessening international tensions. Unesco keeps alive " invisible bridges of understanding," as May Sarton refers to them, and has furthermore started many exciting educational and cultural projects.

(5) They work for the continued separation of church and state. To them this separation is an underlying concept of our country and they exert every effort to keep it so. Children who attend nonsegregated public school systems are relatively free from religious and racial prejudices. In some instances where children have been separated for special released-time religious classes it has been tragic to see the resulting mounting hostilities and class consciousness. Children discover sometimes for the first time that they are Protestant, Catholic, Jewish, or without religious affiliation. And the young humanist is often forced to masquerade as a Protestant, Catholic, or Jew.

(6) They encourage all efforts to increase the world's food supply. It is disheartening to them to see food surpluses destroyed when elsewhere hunger stalks. A controlled economy which destroys these surpluses is not functioning for the benefit of all mankind everywhere.

(7) They work to extend understanding of the values

of planned parenthood. They do not believe in an arbitrarily controlled parenthood but merely in the extension to fathers and to mothers of the right to plan their own families, to have children when they can best take care of them and give them love and security. In two states, Massachusetts and Connecticut, it is still illegal for a physician to give advice of this kind to a woman even though it might save her life. In certain other countries almost no assistance is available to help people have healthy wanted children. The right to plan one's own family has not as yet become a universal right.

(8) They work to improve health services of all kinds and to awaken people to a recognition of the importance of psychological factors. They advocate mental health clinics for they realize that often a little intelligent preventive therapy can avert much suffering and family tragedy.

(9) They have a vigorous interest in continuing and strengthening the free public school system. They resist attempts of special groups to influence public education, whether they be political or religious, business or labor. Opportunities for all children should be offered on the basis of their abilities and not on the basis of the color of their skins or the social background of their parents. Humanists are concerned for the right uses of education. They know that Germany was nearly ruined by the uprising of the ignorant.

These nine fields have one thing in common. They help individuals to enjoy greater freedom and well-being. Yet not all humanists entirely agree on these or any other courses of social action.

It is not specific social action which is the heart of the

humanist approach to social problems. Problems are endless for one can constantly pick out more and more of
them from the flux of human behavior. Application of
the scientific method is what is fundamental.

Humanist Principles That Bear on Social Problems

Let us pause for a moment and consider four principles
which underlie social action.

(1) Humanists believe it is the individual and his welfare which count. By this standard a humanist tests the
value of laws, governments, churches, customs, and other
institutions. All institutions are measured in terms of
the quality of life they promote. They are successful as
they make for better human living.

(2) Humanists express this conviction as to human
value in a strong stand on human equality. They believe
that no race, nationality, or class is innately superior.
No race, nationality, class, or other group " is inherently
qualified to ride herd over any other." As we have said
before, this does not mean that in some areas cultural patterns have not led to differences. Greater equality in living opportunities and conditions lessen these differences.

(3) Humanists are concerned that men be free — free
to think, free to speak as they like, and free to act in-
dependently. They are concerned that no one be
" pushed around " by others. They are opposed to total-
itarianisms which impose arbitrary authority on individual thought and conduct. They are mindful of what
Woodrow Wilson said in New York in 1912:

The history of liberty is a history of the limitations of gov-
ernmental power, not the increase of it. When we resist . . .
concentration of power, we are resisting the powers of death,

because concentration of power is what always precedes the destruction of human liberties.

(4) Humanists are convinced that through cooperation and the intelligent use of science men can create a happier life for all.

These convictions come naturally, of course, to those who believe that there is intrinsic value in men and that human happiness and welfare are the supreme goals. If this life on earth is all we can look forward to, it is unthinkable that we should not make life free from anxieties and richly satisfying. By the use of our resources we can solve most of our problems. That is almost a slogan of humanism.

And because of faith in man's ability to meet his problems, it is natural that the humanist lives vigorously. He knows he must and can depend on the intelligent cooperation of men of good will to continue to remove conditions and change attitudes which breed poverty, hunger, war, disease, fear, and prejudice.

Tackling a Social Problem

A humanist, in tackling a social problem, would use the scientific-democratic method. He would also envision, while remaining open-minded, certain goals which he could look to as a guide and check. These would be the well-being of humankind and concern with individuals as individuals. There are no goals over and beyond these.

To start with, information and points of view are gathered. The most relevant are set apart. Our old friend the scientific method is in high gear.

No matter how emotionally charged the atmosphere, no matter how "close to home" the issue, the humanist

would attempt to look at it freshly, honestly, objectively.
When necessary and desirable he would make a thoroughgoing attempt to search out the opinions of those on dif-
fering sides of the controversy.

He would try to weigh the effects of bias, of limited experience. If one or another solution had been tried elsewhere, he would ascertain how it had worked in practice.
For example, let us say the desirability of changing tariffs
is under discussion. He would consider what actually happened when tariffs were raised or lowered by our own and
other nations. Or again, in considering the treatment of
men in prisons, he would check to find out how other
states handle rehabilitation projects, disciplinary measures,
and parole problems.

The test would be: How has it worked? What have been
the results?

He will attempt to remain open-minded, flexible. He
will face squarely the truth that what works at one place,
at one time, may not work well at another place, at another time. He would be conscious of the complexity of
our human life, in this, the twentieth century. He would
not generalize on such a matter, say, as government own-
ership of gas, water, and electric companies. He would
see that circumstances might make it an excellent policy
in one country and a very questionable one in another.

Because of this flexibility, this dislike of generalizing,
he would not be blocked or upset, for example, by hear-
ing someone allege that such and such a policy is " un-
American." His interest would be in examining into
what the results of such a policy might be. How would
they affect fellow Americans? He knows that words are
dangerous though necessary tools — meaning different

things to different people. Sometimes words, or the meanings hastily applied to them, serve to discourage us from
looking sharply into what is happening, or may happen.

What about those cases where the humanist has little
time to study or reflect, little opportunity to observe at
first hand?

In those cases, he is inclined to suspend judgment, to
make no pronouncement at all. He will have respect for
those who have taken time and pains to investigate, or
who are through training and experience fitted to make
predictions objectively and scientifically.

At this point, someone may wonder whether humanists
believe they have a monopoly on use of the scientific
method in social affairs. Certainly not.

They may, however, have a kind of advantage. For
they hold in mind two things when attacking a problem:
the well-being of all individuals and the necessity of using
the scientific method. People generally tend to be interested in but one or the other of these — or in other goals
entirely.

Faced with making a judgment about a political regime,
a humanist would ask: Are the citizens, as individuals,
subservient to any person, any class, any institutions? Is
there any group of citizens cut off from participating fully
in the life of the country — because of national origin or
membership in any particular class or race?

So far as political party allegiance in our own country
is concerned William Heard Kilpatrick has said:

A humanist may belong to any reputable party, provided
that in his acceptance of this party affiliation he consistently
maintains his respect for human personality and its full devel-

opment, his acceptance of democratic freedom and equality joined with commitment to the common good, and his determination to find out by the free play of intelligence what to think and do as he faces the successive situations of life.

Tackling the Problem of Russia

Most of us will agree that there is one problem today which affects all of us at least indirectly. This is, of course, how the free world should act in relation to the totalitarian Soviet Union. The question is often raised as to what is the humanist's stand on this issue.

In a literal sense, he has none. He could not have as in the case of such debatable questions the opinions of intelligent individuals will always differ.

There are, however, certain points of view which are held by most humanists regarding this question:

(1) Tyranny and oppression, no matter under what name, what banner, are harmful in their effects on men's lives, men's potentialities. Authoritarian and totalitarian governments fail to carry out their duties to citizens.

(2) Soviet communism and humanism are social opposites. The Soviet Union does not permit individual liberty and freedom and does not believe in the primacy of the individual.

(3) Any feeling against Russian communist policy should not involve the assumption that the Russians as a people have inborn irritating traits. They love, hate, desire, and have material needs as do the rest of mankind. Russians are not by nature inherently hostile to us but, like all humans, they act as they are conditioned to act. And the present Russian government — the little group that grabbed power and has imposed arbitrary disciplines

— sees to it that they are conditioned against America and Americans.

(4) The free world should not fall into the comfortable error that it is only Russia which has had interests beyond its borders and therefore is alone in being open to the suspicions of other nations.

(5) For some peoples in other lands the communist promise of security, of food, appears to more than balance the communist threat to liberty. After centuries of oppression, of living under feudalistic conditions, they are promised by the communists that they can have what is rightfully theirs. Accordingly, it is useless for the Western world to speak — to an Indian, for instance — of the joys of theoretical freedom. For centuries he has been beset by the caste system and a rigid feudalism and to him the idea of freedom is vague. But he has learned how miserably poor he is in comparison with most men in the West. To him, talk of enough food to eat is more meaningful than talk of liberty. He listens when he hears that he can become the economic equal of all others and can take part in building a society where exploiters cannot get rich from the work of the poor. He listens when he is told that he can become free from money lenders who charge up to 100 per cent interest annually, and from landlords who extract, in rent, a large part of the crops he grows.

Wherever there are deep-seated, unfulfilled, economic wants and caste systems, wherever there are century-old traditions of entrenched power, wherever it is barely possible for an ordinary man to earn enough to feed his family, the communist story is bound to find listeners.

The need for sufficient food to allay hunger, and for

decent living conditions, is just as deep a need, and just as worthy of respect and concern as the need for liberty. The best defense the free world has against communism is the policy of assisting foreign peoples to satisfy these basic needs, or better still, to help them to help themselves.

CHAPTER EIGHT

The Development of Organization

The American Humanist Association

In 1927 a group of professors and students at the University of Chicago started to publish a mimeographed sheet called *The New Humanist*. The American Humanist Association developed out of this early expression of confidence and faith in man and his future.

In 1929, a humanist club was started in Bangalore, India. Colonel Raja Jai Prithvi Bahadur Singh of Nepal served as the first president of this organization of which Rabindranath Tagore was a member. So far as is known, these Indians were without knowledge of the comparable activity here in the United States.

Before the first World War Unitarian and Universalist churches encouraged on principle freedom of belief among their ministers. After the War these ministers were allowed to express freely any kind of belief from their pulpits and platforms. Liberal ministers whose thought stimulated the development of the organized humanist movement included Curtis W. Reese, M. M. Mangasarian, John Dietrich, Edwin H. Wilson, and Charles Francis Potter. At the same time Percival Chubb, J. Hutton Hynd, and George O'Dell advanced humanist views in Ethical Culture Societies. Another strong impetus came from naturalistic philosophers whose educational theories were widely discussed. John Dewey, Irwin Edman, F. C. S. Schiller, George Santayana, Bertrand Russell, William James, Max Otto, Roy Wood Sellars, and Oliver L. Reiser were among the most influential of these professors. A third contributing trend came from historians and scientists who strongly felt the need for wider recognition of values within a natural framework. Luther Burbank, Robert G. Ingersoll, Thomas Edison, H. S. Jennings, Alfred Korzybski, Harry A. Overstreet, Harry Elmer Barnes, J. B. S. Haldane, Julian Huxley, James Harvey Robinson, C. Judson Herrick, Cassius J. Keyser, Edwin G. Conklin, George Sarton, Lancelot Hogben, and A. Eustace Haydon were noteworthy in this respect. Still another impetus came from literary figures including Walt Whitman, Mark Twain, H. G. Wells, Van Wyck Brooks, George Bernard Shaw, Sinclair Lewis, John Galsworthy, Anatole France, and Jules Romains.

The year 1933 was important for it was then that more than thirty intellectual leaders signed the Humanist Manifesto. Now that document is sometimes considered somewhat dated, but its basic notions, though limited, are acknowleged as sound. When the Manifesto was issued the signers insisted that it was not a creed — only an effort to express their points of agreement at the moment.

Other summaries of the humanist position have been made from time to time. One of these, *Scientific Humanism: A Formulation*, written by Oliver L. Reiser and one of the present authors, attracted relatively little attention when it was published in 1943. Its emphases on basic semantics and on global planning had not as yet been of wide interest to humanists. The mainstream of humanist advance now makes this formulation more timely than ever.

The group which launched *The New Humanist* became known as the New Humanist Associates and organized The Humanist Press Association, expecting to pattern it on The Rationalist Press Association in England. In 1934 the name was changed to the American Humanist Association. Later the association was incorporated as an educational and religious organization, which role it still plays.

The leaders of the American Humanist Association during the 1930's and early 1940's were largely men with other liberal religious affiliations. Serving successively as presidents were E. Burdette Backus, Raymond B. Bragg, J. Hutton Hynd, and Curtis W. Reese. As the organization increased in scope and influence it became necessary to have a full-time executive director and an adequate staff. So in 1949 Edwin H. Wilson was asked to be its first full-time executive. Dr. Wilson and his wife Janet had long been identified with the organized humanist movement. For twenty years he had done organizational and editorial work on a volunteer basis. The legal ability and wisdom contributed over the years by Oswell G. Treadway has been of inestimable value in corporate and organizational matters. Now the American Humanist Association is able to receive bequests. These bequests make it possible better to serve the religious, philosophical, and educational needs of more people.

In recent years the Board and Officers have become more representative of the expanding membership.

These directors now include scientists, businessmen, lawyers, a psychiatrist, and a housewife — Vashti McCollum. It was Mrs. McCollum who almost singlehandedly carried a case to the Supreme Court and there won a decision reaffirming the principle that sectarian religious instruction has no place in the public school room.

Field representatives are coming to play a more important part in the development of the Association. These men and women serve on a volunteer basis and help coordinate the activities of the groups in their area.

Very often where there is a field representative in an urban center, chapters or Humanist study groups have resulted in part through his efforts. Those who have done this include E. Stuart MacDonald, Toronto; W. Howard Beach, Rochester; Roy Everett, Seattle; William H. Stalnaker, Houston; George Paps, Toledo; Sonia Rogolsky, Detroit; B. B. Stoller, Duluth; Warren Allen Smith, New York; and Irving Zaret, Washington D.C. In Chicago Frederick W. Young is making a solid contribution. In rural areas other field representatives such as Wesley Dudgeon carry humanist literature to smaller towns. Several times field representatives have continued their work while in military service, distributing reading material to fellow service men.

The American Humanist Association is chiefly an organization of individuals living throughout the United States and Canada. Affiliated with it, however, are numerous chapters, fellowships, and study groups.

Notable in the chapters that are now rapidly organizing is the presence of mature young people in their twenties. Youth, let down by the religious and political orthodoxies of left and right, repelled by the antiscientific irrationalities of traditional faiths, is looking for a cause to which it can constructively devote itself and is finding that cause in humanism.

There has been little effort to make the organization a tightly-knit one, for it has been felt that one of its major purposes is that of stimulating humanists wherever they may be, and there is a significant and growing number within liberal churches. Humanists are coming to recognize the need for a strong organization but are proceeding with caution so as to avoid any undesirable features of a church or cult.

In a recent letter Edwin H. Wilson said:

Whereas rationalism and freethought has in America tended to develop into a multiplicity of little "one-man groups," the A. H. A. has for a quarter of a century been deliberately working in the direction of a broad organization developing out of the ideas and loyalties and sacrifices of many people. Now with a responsible board, the beginnings of an extension staff of field representatives, and multiplying chapters it has real roots in the commitments of more and more persons. It has been building soundly. At the same time it has resisted efforts to make a " church " out of it in any dogmatic or traditional sense. The aim of humanist publishing has been to keep the movement critical and creative.

In each of the past five years the American Humanist Association has had a healthy increase in membership and in range of activities. In 1953 a " Humanist of the Year " was designated for the first time. This honor went to Anton J. Carlson, the physiologist and former president of the American Association for the Advancement of Science.

It is expected that before long millions of those without any religious affiliation will find in this movement inspiration and strength. This does not imply that all of these humanists will necessarily become members of the Association. We hope that these like-minded individuals will continue to find one another and come together in local groups. The American Humanist Association whose headquarters is in Yellow Springs, Ohio, has information about various groups throughout the country. Assistance in planning regional conferences can also be obtained from the office in Yellow Springs.

The Association's Publications

The Association has three kinds of publications. There is a membership bulletin called *The Free Mind* which discusses activities of largely organizational interest as well as timely comments on human affairs. There is the recently resumed Humanist Press and a projected series of pamphlets, the first of which, George Simpson's *Science as Morality*, has been published. And, most important, there is the bi-monthly *The Humanist*, which can be obtained by subscription and is carried on some newsstands. On the pages of this lively magazine is material that can be found nowhere else. Many world figures contribute to it.

Warren Allen Smith, writing in *The Humanist*, has said:

Naturalistic Humanism, since the start of the century, has attracted an increasing number of the world's thinkers until it now has become recognized as a major philosophy, one involving a socio-political, aesthetic, and scientific outlook upon life. Numbered among its adherents are well-known scientists, political scientists, clergymen, writers, and educators, as well as many leading influential citizens in communities throughout the nation.

In the issue from which this was quoted were comments by Thomas Mann, Stuart Chase, Arthur Koestler, Harry A. Overstreet, Robinson Jeffers, Archibald MacLeish, Rupert Hughes, Conrad Aiken, Witter Bynner, and an article by James Peter Warbasse, founder of the American cooperative movement and a leading humanist.

Columns in *The Humanist* have included Harold Larrabee's " Reliable Knowledge," Edwin H. Wilson's " The Sectarian Battlefront," Maurice B. Visscher's " Science for Humanity," Gerald Wendt's " Science Notes," and a column on race relations written at different times by Homer Jack, Robert Kelso, and Lewis A. McGee.

We agree with the late Eduard C. Lindeman, noted social worker, who said:

> I like *The Humanist* because of its honesty, its audacity, and its sprightliness. I am weary of intellectual double talk, willful confusions, and artful deceptions. So, when *The Humanist* arrives . . . I say to myself, " Here is your chance to communicate with persons who place truth above all other values."

Annually *The Humanist* conducts a Short Story Contest for college undergraduates. Harper & Brothers and G. P. Putnam and Sons have cooperated in this. This project receives the special attention of David McEldowney, the brilliant young managing editor of the bi-monthly.

The First International Congress on Humanism and Ethical Culture

Humanists from many parts of the world gathered together for a humanist conference for the first time in 1952. J. P. van Pragg, Mrs. H. A. Polak-Schwarz, and J. Bijleveld of the outstanding Dutch organization, the Humanistisch

Verbond, were largely responsible for the arrangements of the Conference.

From these meetings held August 21–26 in Amsterdam, Holland, emerged the International Humanist and Ethical Union, which is dedicated to cultivation of science, loyalty to democratic principles, and furtherance of human values without reliance upon authority or dogma.

The several hundred humanists gathered in Amsterdam channeled their discussions into the following areas: The meaning of science and democracy in human progress, the humanization of man in society, and the program of humanism and ethical culture.

In Rudolf Dreikurs' paper presented at the conference, he said:

> The humanist movement may well become the springboard for a new universal religion without acquiring the attributes of a cult. As such, humanism can provide a philosophy which can be a creed, ethics which can be a code, and fellowship cultivating loyalty. It can break down the emotional isolation in which people live in a competitive society, merging each into the whole of his community, into the whole of mankind.

The conference was conducted in both English and in French, which necessarily slowed the tempo at times. Of great interest to the delegates were the slightly different emphases of those from various countries. The Dutch on the whole objected to calling humanism a religion, preferring the terms faith, philosophy, or viewpoint. Some English delegates desired a more fully developed philosophical basis as well as recognition of humanism's social implications. The Americans could hardly have been said to have had any major area of emphasis or agreement. The Belgians were much concerned about freedom from religion in the schools. The Germans were hopeful that they would be recognized as integral parts of the international fight for freedom on all fronts. The French were primarily concerned with protection and furtherance of personal liberty. They had vivid recollections of what it meant to have lost a measure of it. There was a common bond among these delegates of many nations, a bond which ties the present with the future.

The conference commended the work of Unesco, endorsed the Universal Declaration of Human Rights, the Genocide Convention, and the European Convention for the Protection of Human Rights and Fundamental Freedoms as essential steps toward international justice and decency in a free world. Full support was voted the World Conference on Planned Parenthood meeting in Bombay and the World Federation of Mental Health meeting in Brussels.

The Amsterdam Conference Statement

The now famous Fifth Resolution passed at the Conference is well worth quoting in full. The original version of this Resolution was drafted by Hector Hawton. The adopted version has less emotional bite than the original, but it was the result of the deliberations of many minds:

This congress is a response to the widespread demand for an alternative to the religions which claim to be based on revelation on the one hand, and totalitarian systems on the other. The alternative offered as a third way out of the present crisis of civilization is Humanism, which is not a new sect, but the outcome of a long tradition that has inspired many of the world's thinkers and creative artists and given rise to science itself. Ethical Humanism unites all those who cannot any longer believe the various creeds and are willing to base their conviction on respect for man as a spiritual and moral being. The fundamentals of modern, ethical Humanism are as follows:

1. *It is democratic.* It aims at the fullest possible development of every human being. It holds that this is a matter of right. The democratic principle can be applied to all human relationships and is not restricted to methods of government.

2. *It seeks to use science creatively, not destructively.* It advocates a world-wide application of scientific method to problems of human welfare. Humanists believe that the tremendous problems with which mankind is faced in this age of transition can be solved. Science gives the means but science itself does not propose ends.

3. *Humanism is ethical. It affirms the dignity of man and the right of the individual to the greatest possible freedom of development compatible with the rights of others.* There is a danger that in seeking to utilize scientific knowledge in a complex society individual freedom may be threatened by the very impersonal machine that has been created to save it. Ethical Humanism, therefore, rejects totalitarian attempts to perfect the machine in order to obtain immediate gains at the cost of human values.

4. *It insists that personal liberty is an end that must be combined with social responsibility in order that it shall not be sacrificed to the improvement of material conditions.* Without intellectual liberty, fundamental research, on which progress must in the long run depend, would not be possible. Humanism ventures to build a world on the free person responsible to society. On behalf of individual freedom humanism is undogmatic, imposing no creed upon its adherents. It is thus committed to education free from indoctrination.

5. *It is a way of life, aiming at the maximum possible fulfillment, through the cultivation of ethical and creative living.* It can be a way of life for everyone everywhere if the individual is capable of the responses required by the changing social order. The primary task of humanism today is to make men aware in the simplest terms of what it can mean to them and what it commits them to. By uti-

lizing in this context and for purposes of peace the new power which science has given us, humanists have confidence that the present crisis can be surmounted. Liberated from fear the energies of man will be available for a self-realization to which it is impossible to forsee the limit. Ethical humanism is thus a faith that answers the challenge of our times. We call upon all men who share this conviction to associate themselves with us in this cause.

Cooperation among Protestants, Catholics, Jews, and Humanists

A Sunday does not pass in which some clergyman does not attack humanism as godless atheism, worship of man, or the handiwork of the devil. These attacks are reminiscent of those leveled fifty years ago by various religious leaders against men of other faiths. Gradually these religious leaders have come to believe it is no longer desirable to persecute those of a different major religion. This gives comfort to the humanist who is now subjected to criticism. He knows that these false accusations will be refuted by increased knowledge of what humanists actually think and actually do.

A growing number of liberal Protestant ministers, rabbis, and ex-Catholic priests are openly speaking as humanists. These men are turning their emphasis from man's relation to God to man's relation with his fellows. The enthusiasm of these religious leaders is bound to carry over into practically all denominations.

A few ministers are suggesting that humanism is but Christianity in action. This is not entirely without justification for the application of ethical principles can be made without any attention to theology, traditional religious observances, or consideration of man's relation to

God.   These same ministers sometimes say that Christianity is "humanism plus." Humanists do not consider this to be any more accurate than designating humanism as "Christianity plus." Humanism applies the scientific method to all phases of man's life — ethical and spiritual as well as social and physical.   Adherents of the four faiths have the same concern for ideals and the welfare of all individuals.   The humanist differs from those in the three other faiths in the conviction that the methods used have to be consistently scientific.

CHAPTER NINE

The Great Adventure

How to Decide Whether You Are a Humanist

Several writers have worked out questionnaires by which one can tell whether or not one can be classified as a humanist. It is with some reluctance that we offer still another set of questions.

(1) Do you believe that men will continue to learn more about the way the earth was formed, life developed, and how men have created their ethical and moral systems?

(2) Do you believe that men are a part of nature and that there is no deity especially concerned for their welfare?

(3) Do you believe that the religions of the world and the sacred scriptures were the creations of mortal men and that religions have served different purposes at different times and places?

(4) Do you believe that the kind of life we live and the kind of relationship that we have with other humans is of primary importance?

(5) Do you believe that psychologists, psychiatrists, and social scientists will continue to add to our knowledge of the conditions of individual and social well-being?

(6) Do you frequently experience zest and contentment from the realization that you are a part of nature?

(7) Do you believe that the meaning of life is that which we give to it?

If you answer " yes " to most of these questions you can classify yourself as a humanist for you view men in naturalistic and humanist terms. You have faith in man's future here on earth and believe the highest goal for human endeavor is a better world for all men.

Are you willing to consider new evidence of any kind and in every field of human thought and behavior, even though this may lead to a revision of some of your most cherished beliefs? We cannot see how anyone who is consistent in his belief in a theistic religion or a nonnaturalistic philosophy is able to answer this in the affirmative. Humanists can.

For Sober Reflection

We all know that in some ways man's inner resources are not keeping pace with his external ones. Each year sees more machines and devices bringing added leisure and comfort to millions of people. Yet little seems to be achieved in helping men to be basically happier or wiser. Even among those with countless machine-age gadgets and abundant leisure there is often ennui, a sense of futility and worthlessness.

What is wrong? The explanation most frequently given is that men do not follow Christianity, Mohammedanism, or whatever the religion happens to be. Say the theologically-minded, " If only people would come to know God, if only they would accept Him on faith and not question or hold back! "

The humanist thinks otherwise. He appreciates and gladly accepts the values of the historical ethical codes.

He notes, however, that these very old codes contain views on slavery, the position of women, and other matters which are not acceptable to contemporary men and women. Then, too, there are countless situations upon which the old codes do not provide guidance. The humanist feels hopeful that our inner growth will be greater when the same methods that have made scientific achievements possible are used by ourselves in our own personal development and social relations. He believes the remedy is in looking forward, not backward, in observation and experience, in free imagination, in studying consequences of action, and not in dependence upon revelation and tradition. To date there has been no nation which has put into general practice, the scientific method — the humanist method — whereas whole nations have been Christianized or galvanized behind other major philosophies and religions. The Christian ideals are admirable, but more than the voice of revelation is needed to make them living realities.

In some ways humanism is little more than the carrying over into religious and ethical life of the general scientific approach. In the practical routines of daily life people are often distrustful of pronouncements, for they gather evidence and check facts before making decisions. For the ideals of the great religions to be more nearly achieved here on this earth and in our own lifetime we might well use this approach in ethics, morals, and religion. Toward this end the humanist labors, loves, and adventures. Many people, we believe, are ready to make this transition.

What Humanism Gives Us

Humanism serves as both an inspiring religion and an adequate philosophy for daily living. This sparkling faith, this way of life, is richly rewarding and deeply satisfying.

We see ourselves as a dynamic part of nature, responding to the same laws as do other creatures. We observe the working of these natural laws finding no need to set ourselves apart from the world or to project our various human purposes or plans onto the grand cosmic scheme of things.

Depressing negatives have been turned into challenging positives. What if we are the result of evolutionary change from lower animals? We can feel pride and responsibility in being the highest form of life that has as yet evolved — the spearhead of evolution!

What if the vast universe is neutral toward our human hopes, our human ideals? We are still free to carve out our own plans, set our own standards. Each of us is free to give whatever meaning he wishes to his or her life. Moreover, with increasing knowledge we learn more of nature's laws and how to cooperate with them more fully. The ideals of the great religions can more nearly become living realities. As B. B. Stoller said at the 1953 Midwest Regional Conference of the American Humanist Association:

Humanism does offer a faith, based on science, in the creative potentialities of man, a faith in the dignity, gentleness, and creativity of man.

Many find in the fourth faith a satisfying philosophy and religion which does not run counter to their knowledge of the world. For them new vistas have been opened. New possibilities for human cooperation in making a heaven on earth have been presented. It is the youth of today who are accepting the challenge and opportunity to develop this faith. When there are sufficient numbers of humanists in the world a new day will surely arrive. From here until there it is a long, hard, difficult trail. Yet in following it anyone can enjoy the greatest of human adventures.

Albert Schweitzer, man of international good will now living in Africa and recipient of the Nobel Peace Prize for 1952, has said:

The world thinks it must raise itself above humanism; that it must look for a more profound spirituality. It has taken a false road. Humanism in all its simplicity is the only genuine spirituality. Only ethics and religion which include in themselves the humanitarian ideal have true value. And humanism is the most precious result of rational meditation upon our existence and that of the world.

Appendix

In 1950 the American Humanist Association sponsored a World Humanism Essay Contest open to any who were not American citizens. The response was gratifying, and essays were received from all over the world — from Africa, Asia, Australia, Europe, and the Americas.

The winning essay was written by a gifted Englishman, Hector Hawton, editor of the Rationalist Press Association and of Watts & Co. Mr. Hawton is also the author of philosophical books and of mystery stories. His essay, "Humanism: The Third Way," appeared in the December 1951 issue of The Humanist. *We are reprinting it here because it gives with great clarity a picture of the humanist movement as many Europeans see it. Across the Atlantic humanism is often regarded as an alternative system of belief to Christianity and to Communism. Thought of in this way, it becomes more than a philosophy or a religion. It becomes in every sense of the word a way of life. Those who follow this way of life are distinguished by their faith in freedom and in science from those who follow the twin orthodoxies.*

Humanism: The Third Way

BY HECTOR HAWTON

Many people feel that in the present crisis of civilization they must choose between Christianity and Communism. They do not realize that by stating the issue in such simple terms they are succumbing to the logic of the very authoritarianism they fear. Both Christianity and Communism are authoritarian systems. Both impose a rigid theory and a way of life from above; private judgment is subordinated to scriptural text, or church discipline, or to the party line. Both claim to be in possession of certain truths, to deny which would be held impious or treasonable. The history of the Christian Church — whether Protestant or Catholic — shows to what extreme lengths otherwise kindly men will go in suppressing opposition, when they believe they have attained certitude. And we know from recent events that Communism is even more ruthless (and a great deal more efficient) in extirpating heresy. The reason that, despite these facts, the modern dilemma is so often seen as a choice between Christianity and Communism is partly due to the success of propaganda, partly to the difficulty of seeing a third choice.

Propaganda, making capital of a widespread weariness of mere argument, skillfully uses the logical fallacy popularized by Existentialists. This is the time for decision,

we are told. We cannot sit on the fence forever; we must
come down on one side or the other. And this very anal-
ogy tacitly assumes there are only two choices. It is as if
we were told to choose between black and white, disregard-
ing the possibility of any other color. If we object, we
are met with another argument, similar in form: " He
who is not with us is against us." This suggests that if
we ally ourselves with Christians in a struggle against
Communism, we support Christianity " objectively." It
means, in effect, the original challenge still holds: " Either
Christianity or Communism." But a moment's reflection
shows that in such a struggle we may also find ourselves
in alliance with Mohammedans, Hindus, Buddhists and
Jews. The " either-or " fallacy is the source of a dangerous
confusion of thought, and those who accept it sweep aside
the right of independent minorities to assert themselves.
Such right is of the essence of democracy; and that is why
Humanism, itself a minority movement, can only survive
in a democratic society. On this side of the Iron Curtain,
at least, Humanism, though it may be frowned upon, is
tolerated. Even the Catholic Church, the most totalitarian
form of Christianity, without abating one jot of its theoretical right to persecute, tolerates the existence of Humanism in practice. But on the other side of the Iron
Curtain, Humanism is not allowed to show itself. It is
denounced as " Westernism " or " decadent bourgeois lib-
eralism," and its exponents suffer the fate of " lackeys of
American Imperialism."

In the present state of the world there can be no question whatever about the alignment of Humanism. It is
part and parcel of the free, democratic world. In order
to change admitted evils in the democratic world, Human-

ism must support, in the last analysis, a social framework that at least permits shortcomings to be exposed. The first duty of Humanism is to survive; to align itself with a frankly totalitarian regime would be suicidal.

In comparison to its great rivals, Humanism is a soul without a body, a stream of ideas without their effective organization. The absence of any striking, visible embodiment is no doubt one reason why it is overlooked by many who long to find an alternative to Christianity — in which they cannot believe — and to Communism — which they do not want. Nor is there any philosophic system or any program of action commanding wide agreement that can confidently be denoted Humanist. " I can see tables, but not tabularity," complained Diogenes to a Platonist. And so we can point to a long succession of Humanists from the Sixth Century B.C. onward; but we cannot select a unique system and say that it is, without question, Humanism.

The pressure of the great crisis of civilization through which we are passing will remedy this state of affairs. Already the demand for an international organization which will represent and clarify what is broadly meant by " Humanist " thought is making itself felt. Julian Huxley failed in his attempt to make " Scientific Humanism " the official philosophy of Unesco; but the majority of scientific workers, as well as a large educated public, would probably be found to be in sympathy with such a philosophy if it were clearly formulated. The urgent duty of the rudimentary organization that is taking shape on two continents is to re-state in modern idiom the basic principles of the great Humanist tradition. We cannot hope to rally potential supporters until we have made it plain what we stand for and what we propose to offer in place of Christianity, on the one hand, and Communism, on the other.

This is obviously no easy task, because Humanism is distinguished from authoritarian systems in that it offers no absolutely certain truths. It actually encourages nonconformity. Humanism would be false to its own nature if it drew up a final and dogmatic set of propositions and demanded that they should be accepted. The Humanist does not impose dogmas but incites men to embark on the voyage of intellectual discovery and to accept only what they themselves have tested and found reasonable. In this quest for knowledge, however, the philosophy provides the most powerful of all navigational aids: the scientific method.

It cannot be disputed that of all the various ways in which man has sought to increase his knowledge, the discipline of science has been overwhelmingly the most successful. In three hundred years, science has transformed our entire outlook on the universe and man's place in it. For the modern Humanist, science must be the starting point of any philosophy. If we venture beyond the findings of the special sciences and try to work out a speculative scheme, we do so at the risk of talking nonsense. On matters remote from verification, the inclination of the Humanist is to be cautious and tentative in expressing an opinion; and we must admit that many different opinions can be legitimately held. In other words, in the realm of pure philosophy Humanism has many mansions, and the problem is to fix the limits within which we may differ. Humanism, for example, cannot include the philosophies of Aquinas or Marx without losing its distinctive character. It is more than doubtful whether contemporary Humanism can accommodate Heidegger and Sartre, though room might be found for Jaspers. We can with confidence assign a place to Dewey, Russell, Whitehead and Wittgenstein.

In dealing with such questions even more attention should be paid to the method whereby a philosopher arrives at his conclusions, than to the conclusions themselves. Humanism cannot accept any form of religious revelation and is mistrustful of intuition. It cannot accept the method of deductive rationalism employed by Descartes, Leibnitz and Spinoza. If a system must be built, it must be in the nature of a hypothesis — a provisional scheme of concepts, subject to constant revision, in terms of which a rational interpretation to every element in human experience is sought. But for the fact that " Naturalism " is one of the most ambiguous terms in philosophy, it would have been shorter to say outright that Humanism is Naturalism.

When we come down from this rarefied atmosphere there is much less room for differences. Thus, if we ask ourselves what the outstanding representatives of the Humanist tradition from the time of the Ionians down to the present day have in common, we can see at once that they were all more concerned with the affairs of this world than with the next. In the classical world, there were the various mystery cults. Later on, Christianity promised very special rewards in the hereafter for those who spurned earthly pleasures. The earth was not regarded as man's home; he was a stranger and an exile, and heaven (or hell) was his destination. In contrast, the Humanists took the view that man could attain happiness here and now. Humanists, moreover, did not believe that human nature was essentially depraved. On the contrary, they held that by living in accordance with his true nature, man achieved goodness.

This was no selfish sensualism. The "garden" of Epicurus was a small-holding, where a few displaced persons lived frugally and cultivated peace-of-mind by ridding themselves of superstitious fears and studying the science of the day. The Stoics had a keener social conscience. They had a vision of man, not as a citizen of a small city-state, but of the whole cosmos. If the only armour against Fate seemed to be indifference to its blows, that was because no way of mastering Fate could be seen until modern science gave man a measure of control over what had hitherto seemed inescapable.

The history of societies, as well as of thought, shows that man is both a political and an ethical animal. He is not merely preoccupied with specific codes of conduct, but — as soon as we have any record of abstract thought — he is found to have been concerned with the idea of "right." It may well be that this notion of "right" is indefinable, not capable of further reduction by analysis. But Humanism has shown that "right" does not require the support of supernaturalism. It is rooted in human nature, and that is what we mean by saying that human nature is good and not warped by some supposed Original Sin. Humanists believe that they best fulfill their nature and realize its highest capacity by an act of will when, come what may, they do what they believe to be right.

Modern Humanism is the immediate successor to the Positivist "Religion of Humanity" and to the Ethical movement of the Nineteenth Century. In the 1880's the landslide of Victorian unbelief gave rise to a crop of Ethi-

cal Societies. Some of them still flourish; and though the
Positivist Church is moribund, the modern Humanist
feels, with Gilbert Murray, that what Comte was trying
to say " is not only sublime but true." He was trying to
say that we can lead decent lives, based on sympathetic
understanding of each other's needs, continuously developing man's *Humanitas,* without any belief in a personal
God. And this is not so very different from what one of
the later Stoics had affirmed long before with *Deus est
Mortali iuvare mortalem* (" God is the helping of man by
man").

For the Humanist there is no double-code, as for so
many Christians. He is not saddled with the impracti-
cable, perfectionist ethics of the New Testament, which
sprang from a conviction that the end of the world was at
hand. The end of the world did not come; and the
Church had perforce to develop an ethical system which
could be practiced by those engaged in the administration
of State and Empire. When the medieval order broke
down, there was a tendency for religion and politics to
separate. The function of modern Humanism is to bring
them together; not, obviously, to revive dogmatic religion,
but to insist that ethical principles must guide our decisions in peace and war. The Humanist must ask of any
social enactment the most searching questions — not
merely whether the act is expedient, but whether it is
right.

Science cannot tell us what is right, but it can often
save us from wasting our energies in pursuit of an impossible goal, and it can aid us powerfully in reaching our
goal. For example, it is fashionable at the moment to say
that progress is an illusion; but Humanists agree with

Julian Huxley that, "Progress is a scientific fact." Again, if the theory that certain races are intrinsically inferior to others were true, we should not waste time fighting for equal status; but to the Humanist this is an empirical question to be decided by evidence, and he will heed the recent report prepared by Unesco which states that there is no evidence to support discrimination on racial grounds. In the practical conduct of affairs, the Humanist will be more ready to listen to the trained economist than to the politician; and he will supplant the exorcist by the psychiatrist.

One of the major problems of our time — and one to which governments are tempted to shut their eyes — is that the population of the world is rapidly outstripping the available food supply. The spectre of Malthus has returned. Prayer will not avert this danger; and the resistance to birth-control, based on religious taboos (or, as in the USSR, on the need for a large army) will only aggravate it. The most hopeful immediate line is agricultural research to increase the fertility of the soil and reduce the appalling wastage of our resources, due to erosion and the ravages of pests. A large-scale expansion of the work of the World Health Organization is the best way to accomplish this — and it is the Humanist way.

Looking back, we can see how the range of sympathy has been extended. There was a time when no one cared what happened outside his own clan; then the limits of concern were extended to the city-state, and then to a great empire. Today, the unit is the world. The appeal of Humanism is global. In that, it resembles its great rivals, Communism and Christianity. But in its appeal to unitary man it has the unique advantage of possessing the international language of science. Whatever the country, whatever the race, the same method and the same concepts of science are accepted. The same cannot be said of Christianity; and although Communism protests that it is scientific, the Lysenko incident alone is sufficient to show that science would be stifled in an atmosphere of metaphysical orthodoxy ultimately imposed by force.

Humanism sees in the freedom of thought, only possible in a genuine democracy, an essential condition of civilized life — and in the long run, of the very survival of civilization. Humanism has contributed at least two vital ideals to what are sometimes called " Western Values ": toleration and the disinterested pursuit of truth. Without these virtues — which arose in the teeth of religious opposition — science would be impossible. The springs of discovery and creative thought would dry up. And without the Humanist insistence that ethical principles should control our use of scientific knowledge, science could destroy us.

We stand today at the crossroads. Humanism scorns the counsels of despair and the retreat of frightened men to obscurantism. It offers a way out of the crisis — *the only way*. If Humanist societies are formed in every free country, then federated into a world-movement, we can hope to implement many of our ideas and guide mankind safely through this age of transition. The goal is not an imaginary Utopia, but a sane and ordered society in which men can realize to the full the rich potentialities of their nature.

Suggestions for Further Reading

BOOKS

Burkhardt, Frederick, ed. *The Cleavage in Our Culture: Studies in Scientific Humanism in Honor of Max Otto.* Boston: Beacon Press, 1952.

Chase, Stuart. *The Proper Study of Mankind.* New York: Harper & Brothers, 1948.
Specific examples of science in human relations.

Dewey, John. *A Common Faith.* New Haven: Yale University Press, 1934.

Dewey, John, and Bentley, Arthur F. *Knowing and the Known.* Boston: Beacon Press, 1949.
Tough reading but rewarding.

Fromm, Erich. *Man for Himself.* New York: Rinehart, 1947.

———. *Psychoanalysis and Religion.* New Haven: Yale University Press, 1950.

Hayakawa, S. I. *Language in Thought and Action.* New York: Harcourt, Bruce, 1949.
Useful for everyone.

Huxley, Julian. *Man in the Modern World.* London: Chatto & Windus, 1950.

Keyes, Kenneth S., Jr. *How to Develop Your Thinking Ability.* New York: McGraw-Hill, 1950.
Simple and interesting.

Lamont, Corliss. *Humanism as a Philosophy.* New York: Philosophical Library, 1949.
A fine general survey.

Living as a Humanist. Essays by H. J. Blackham, Virginia Flemming, Ursula Edgcumbe, and M. L. Burnet. London: Chaterson, Ltd. (Obtainable from the American Humanist Association.)
　　Well written though moderately difficult.

Kluckhohn, Clyde. *Mirror for Man: The Relation of Anthropology to Modern Life.* New York: Whittlesey House, 1949.

MacLeish, Archibald. *Freedom Is the Right to Choose.* Boston: Beacon Press, 1951.

May, Rollo. *Man's Search for Himself.* New York: W. W. Norton, 1953.

Mayer, Charles. *Man: Mind or Matter?* Boston: Beacon Press, 1951.

Montagu, Ashley. *On Being Human.* New York: Henry Schuman, 1951.
　　Excellent on the nature of human nature and human relations.

Otto, Max C. *Science and the Moral Life.* New York: New American Library of World Literature, 1949.

Overstreet, H. A. *The Mature Mind.* New York: W. W. Norton, 1949.

Patten, William. *The Grand Strategy of Evolution.* Boston: Richard G. Badger, 1920.
　　The place of cooperation in nature.

Proceedings of the First International Congress on Humanism and Ethical Culture. Utrecht, Netherlands: Humanistisch Verbond, 1953. (Obtainable from the American Humanist Association.)

Reiser, Oliver L. *Nature, Man and God.* Pittsburgh: University of Pittsburgh Press, 1951.

――――. *The Promise of Scientific Humanism.* New York: Oskar Piest, 1940.
　　These two books are for those who like to play with ideas.

Sargent, Porter. *Extending Horizons.* Boston: Porter Sargent, 1950.

Smith, Homer W. *Man and His Gods.* Boston: Little Brown, 1952.
    An intelligent review.

The Thinker's Library, published in London by Watts & Co. (5 & 6 Johnson's Court, Fleet Street, E. C. 4), consists of inexpensive editions containing much outstanding material. Books by humanist authors include *Man Makes Himself,* by V. Gordon Childe; *Man: The Verdict of Science,* by G. N. Ridley; *The Religion of the Open Mind,* by A. Gowans Whyte; *The Origin of the Kiss, and Other Scientific Diversions,* by C. M. Beadnell; and *Religion without Revelation,* by Julian Huxley.

PERIODICALS

The Humanist. Published bi-monthly by the American Humanist Association, Yellow Springs, Ohio.
    Essential reading; includes material found nowhere else.

Manas. P.O. Box 112, El Sereno Station, Los Angeles 32, California.
    A journal of independent inquiry, regarded by some as *The New Yorker* of intellectual magazines.

Etc.: A Review of General Semantics. 539 West North Avenue, Chicago 10, Illinois.
    A quarterly.

Index